For John and Martin

TEACH ME HOW TO CRY was first produced by LPS Productions at the Theater de Lys, New York City, on April 5, 1955. It was staged by Robert Hartung, and the cast was as follows:

MRS. GRANT	Nancy Marchand
MISS ROBSON	Mary James
MELINDA GRANT	Deirdre Owens
POLLY FISHER	Charron Follett
BRUCE MITCHELL	Jack Betts
ANNE	Mildred Trares
ELEANOR	Jane McArthur
WILL HENDERSON	Richard Morse
MRS. HENDERSON	Nan McFarland
MR. HENDERSON	John C. Becher

PARENTS and STUDENTS, Julann Wright, Kathy Dugas, Ted Sturgess, Tom Tyrrell

The action takes place in a small town in America. Spring.

THE STORY OF THE PLAY

TEACH ME HOW TO CRY concerns the manner in which human beings shape one another, and tells the story of a troubled teen-age girl who is steered away from a hazardous life of escapism by the love of a boy who has himself learned to face reality.

Melinda Grant is the illegitimate daughter of a gentle, mildly demented seamstress, living in a small town under the shadow of scandal. She yearns for a mother's love and guidance, for young companionship, for personal identity. This identity she seeks in the role of Juliet in a school production of Romeo and Juliet, and thereby meets Will Henderson.

He also lacks roots, for his father is a travelling salesman; and the constant moving combined with family discord has made the boy insecure and sensitive to rejection. In his loneliness, he writes poetry, and observes with intuitive compassion the needs of others. Will has determined that the best way to come to terms with a world that he does not understand is to peer into the mysteries and devote all his energies to trying to unravel them.

Melinda and Will are drawn together out of mutual need, and together they find their way toward personal dignity and a sense of belonging. At their trysting place, a burnt-out bandstand on a hill overlooking the town, there grows between them the first real love and companionship of their lives. Melinda has formed the habit of protecting herself against hurt by turning away from reality and suppressing all emotion; but under the influence of Will's tenderness and understanding, she releases into laughter and tears. From his strength, she gains courage; from his love, how to give love in return.

The love story parallels that of Romeo and Juliet. The two young lovers struggle against parental opposition and the pressures of society, to the point where Will becomes involved in a fight, and is punished by banishment . . . expulsion from school, and from the town.

But the two young people have gained sufficient strength and courage to endure the separation. Melinda has acquired a realistic view of her relationship with her mother, and is prepared to withstand her mother's attempts to draw her into her own life of fantasy.

She and Will begin to plan their future together, for, unlike the classic lovers, they see their answer in Life instead of Death.

SET AND PRODUCTION NOTES

The set is in four sections, and is not changed throughout the play. Each section is lit as we use it and the others remain in darkness.

Upstage is a raised platform extending almost the entire width of the stage. This is the scene of the ruins of the Bandstand. There need be just a suggestion of the ruins of a small bandstand, the extent of the surrounding hilltop depending on the resources and imagination of the designer. A few steps lead up to the bandstand. The bandstand is slightly to L. of C. and R. of it is a small stone bench which will seat two people. The platform for the bandstand need not be very high if the proscenium does not permit.

Downstage C. is a small section with no scenery, the locale of which will change as we require it. The area will be assumed to be a school terrace in Act I, Scene 2, and a school corridor in Act II, Scene 3. There should be two small low sections of wall to suggest a center entrance. There are two small benches at R. and L. D. C., forward of the entrance.

Downstage R. is the Henderson kitchen. There is an entrance at R. A coat hook is on the wall near the entrance. A stove and sink U. C. in front of a window. D. S. of the sink is a waste basket. U. R. is an icebox and D. R. some shelves. On the shelves are bowls, cooking utensils and some magazines. A table and three chairs are grouped C.

Downstage L. is the Grant Living Room. The room has one entrance, U. L., leading from a small hall, which contains a table and wall mirror. The front door and hall should be visible to the audience, and can be at far L. of set. In the original production the hall extended from L. to R. behind the living room, and could be seen because the back living room wall was transparent . . . built of screening and covered with a gauze material simulating wallpaper. There is a small Victorian sofa C., with a small three-tiered tea rack in front of it. One chair at R., by a window R. which faces the center section of the stage itself. Curtains hang at the window. There is a collection of dolls, beautifully dressed, on a what-not rack against wall at R. A side table is against D. L. wall.

Neither the Henderson kitchen nor the Grant living room should have more depth than is necessary for movement, in order that the action on the bandstand will not be too far removed from the audience.

An illusion of greater space can be attained by playing out a little into the D. C. section during the Grant and Henderson scenes, and vice versa. The chair R. in the Grant living room, on which Miss Robson sits, can be out a little into the D. C. section, and can be lifted back into the living room during the blackout at the end of the first scene.

In fact, as the chair is not used again, it may be removed from the stage during the first act intermission, and so leave more space for movement in the later living room scenes. The Henderson kitchen table should be well U. R. during the first two scenes of the play, and lifted down into position during the blackout following Act I, Scene 2. It will be moved up again during the first act intermission, and down during the second act intermission. The two benches which are used D. C. in Act I, Scene 2 may be carried on during the blackout following the first scene.

TEACH ME HOW TO CRY was originally designed as a two act play, and was divided into three acts in the original production, because the tiny stage of the Delys Theatre prohibited the use of the multiple set; the six scenes, with curtain and set changes, made the second act appear too lengthy. However, the author strongly advises the use of the multiple set to maintain flow and continuity. The action of the play is essentially emotional rather than physical, and it is permissible to have the sections of the set very small. The two act form might then be experimented with, for it is undesirable to break the mood of the play more than once. The first act would remain as is, and the present acts two and three would comprise a single act.

In designing the set, a great range of flexibility may be exercised. The design may range from detailed realism, through mere suggestion, to bare stage. If the play is done on a bare stage, a few necessary props should be used. The dolls, a suggested window frame, chairs and an occasional table, a few planks on boxes for the steps of the bandshell, and the benches. The author's belief is that a halfway measure should be found, using imaginative suggestion, and keeping in mind that the simplicity of the story is best enhanced by simple sets and dramatic lighting.

In the New York production the play was set in 1919, which provided opportunity for interesting costumes and decor and contributed a feeling of other-world nostalgia. However, the change is not necessary, as the play was written for modern dress, and will doubtless have a quality of its own if presented in a modern day setting.

The music can conceivably be dispensed with, but it is very valuable if at all possible. If the music is live, it should be a cornet or trumpet, played well away in the distance, with a sad and melting quality suggestive of subconscious memory traces rather than actuality. If it is necessary to choose a recording, a full band should be avoided. It should be possible to find a section of single brass from either band or classical music.

If the multiple set is not employed, the pantomime following Act III, Scene 2, should be eliminated, and the action should go right from the bandstand to the Grant living room.

NOTES ON CHARACTERS

Melinda

Melinda never smiles, nor does she cry, nor in any way openly express emotion. At a casual meeting one would think of her as possessing great composure; but a closer look reveals the tension that poses as calm. If Melinda had *given in* to starvation, she would have the real quietude of the walking dead, but her tension is due to the striving spirit within her which craves love and an area of belonging.

And so in the playing she must not be represented as "toneless and expressionless," but must illustrate the conflict that rages within her, by an outward appearance of rigid control and at the same time an inner yearning that verges on desperation. She has not stopped feeling emotions, she has just stopped showing them.

She has had to find a way to protect herself from attack, and so has built around herself a wall of iron behind which she withdraws at the slightest sign of approach. She does not consider whether the approach might be friendly, for she has never experienced such a thing as friendliness. Her withdrawal is so automatic that by now there is no way to get to her. The only way through the wall is from the *inside*. It is during her first meeting with Will that she senses a troubled spirit like her own, and of her own volition, out of her tortured need for communication, she reaches out very tentatively toward him. This creates a slight chink in the wall, which she tries to seal up again with "I don't want to be taught" . . . but it is too late. Will has seized the advantage and has begun his invasion of the fortress.

The emotion that must be roused in the audience toward Melinda is compassion . . . not pity. If she herself indulges in self pity, we will pity her, and of course we cannot really like anyone whom we pity. But the picture of her indomitable spirit, fighting strongly against overwhelming odds, and the hard control she has mastered, will rouse in us admiration and sorrow, and hence, real compassion.

Her performance throughout the play may be termed a gradual process of "relaxation of suppression." But at no point is she uninhibitedly joyous. Never is her smile (when, under the influence of love, she smiles) completely free, for she is unpracticed at happiness. A restraint governs all her flowering emotions, with the exception of the play's climax, when she "cries right out."

Her entire growth in the play is directed toward the moment when she realizes Will is going away. Then all her impulses are toward a return to rigidity. We must feel the old tension grip her, the determination to reveal no emotion, to protect herself against this hurt by allowing herself to feel nothing. We must see the fight between these impulses and the new courage of expression that Will has been teaching her throughout the play. This is the supreme struggle. Courage wins . . . and she cries . . . and is made human. The crying, if done freely, with total release, will indicate more of joyousness than heartbreak.

The tenderness that Melinda displays for her mother at the final curtain will be meaningless unless we have clearly felt her hostility toward her mother in the early part of the play. Always it is restrained, and without intent to hurt, but it is understandably present. The hostility has been gradually draining out of her during her association with Will, and it ends suddenly when her mother mentions the word "love" in the final moments of the play. Melinda is shaken by the sudden rush of tenderness that she feels. She seems to stop breathing as she starts across the room for the doll. Now she can afford to please her mother by identifying with the dolls, because she has found, securely, her own identity.

Mrs. Grant

Mrs. Grant is not insane, nor should she be portrayed as even "touched." When we first see her, we see a person who appears to be merely pleasant. But soon we sense an unnaturalness about the pleasantness, for it is maintained with constancy and iron determination. She is gentle, but inexorable. Her entire being strains toward the shelter of "niceness," and is acutely sensitive to the slightest hint of tension or trouble.

Terror lived in this house with her from the day she was born. She existed in a climate of brutality, rejection and heartbreak, until the day of the final crush, when the man on whom she had showered all the saved-up love of her life betrayed her. On that day she simply turned her back on reality, which to her was total blackness, and went out into the sunlight and is determined to stay there. She is not vague, she is precise. She knows what she wants. She wants the day without the night, sun without shadow, pretty happiness without substance.

She does not think, she feels. Her responses are rapid, since they are based on the instinct of self-preservation. She knows where Reality is . . . it stands solid and immovable, a pillar of Terror; and she has learned to veer around it with the speed and silence of a ghost. Through the years she has got it placed, and knows exactly how to avoid it. It is when the Terror turns up in unexpected places and she runs into it, that she panics.

No real tenderness exists between her and her daughter. To Mrs. Grant, Melinda is a doll. Or she would like her to be a doll, for one can love a doll and it makes no demands. We can assume that she cared for the baby Melinda with the on-again off-again affection of a child for its plaything. She would rock the baby tenderly, then put her aside in boredom and forget to feed her. Melinda's sense of deprivation is deeply rooted, and hence her hostility toward her mother.

Mrs. Grant once had a tremendous capacity for love (had she been less sensitive and loving she might better have withstood the rigors of her life); and even now there is a deep longing for it. She has so completely escaped from life that she would no longer know how to give love in return, but her need of it is primary and basic, as the need of an infant. "If you love me, you will not let me be hurt." She senses Melinda's hostility, is made tired by the necessity for increased effort to escape Melinda's demands for mothering. At the end of the play, when Melinda, having found a source of love and strength, sees her mother with sympathy and tenderness, Mrs. Grant's fears gently sigh and are put to rest. She feels the presence of love in the house now, and with it protection. She is warmed and enveloped by the sun.

. . . .

In the playing of Melinda and Mrs. Grant, notice should be taken of the fact that certain words have great meaning for them. For Mrs. Grant, "nice" and "love" and "friend" have a light around them, and the word "hate" elicits a violent inner turmoil. It is a forbidden word in this house.

When Melinda uses the words "hate" and "terrible," we must see a black cloud quietly gather, for they symbolize the girl's tortured rebellion against the niceness that has starved and nearly destroyed her.

WILL

Will is a poet and a realist. It is not such an odd combination, for the modern poet finds beauty in reality, and it is well known that the artist and the scientist are driven by the same basic integrative drive.

We can trace the beginnings of Will's development as a realist to the episode of the deserted house down by the lake. A sensitive insecure boy, haunted by fears, doubtless tempted toward escape by the example of his mother, was forced by circumstances to face up to reality. In the final Bandstand Scene he recalls with vivid feeling the torment of the occasion, and imparts to Melinda a measure of the courage that he gained by "looking at it, every bit of it, up close."

After his experience of facing the ghosts of the old house, we can assume that he began to examine other fears and mysteries with his newly opened eyes and awakened courage, and slowly, laboriously, found his way toward knowledge. His innate tenderness and compassion have since been enhanced by the real and deep understanding that he has of other human beings; understanding gained through perseverance and enforced loneliness, through thwarted love of humanity, and his own need for something certain to cling to.

The sureness and strength, then, that he exhibits in certain areas, are derived from the solid truths that he has discovered. They are few in number, but many of them are important truths, and once found, they do not desert him.

But apart from the isolated security it has given him, he has never had a chance to put his knowledge to real use. He is like the artist or the scientist, working in solitude, awaiting the final proof that comes only with practical application. The world spins by him; when he can observe the maelstrom from a safe distance, he can snatch at and capture bits of meaning, but when he is swept up into the social current he finds himself awkward, aggressive and uncertain. He has been uprooted so many times that he has formed only fleeting associations with people. He knows how to observe, but he does not know how to behave.

And so when we first see him with Polly, we think him every bit as gauche and objectionable as does she. It is during his ensuing conversation with Melinda that his confidence begins to emerge, for he has found someone impassive and undemanding. With her, he has the same certainty of opinion that he feels when he is alone.

His desire to help Melinda does not spring to life immediately, but grows as he grows in security with her, and is then free to sense her need. At first he is driven mainly by an impulse to prove himself. It is at the First Act Curtain, when he realizes that she does not "cry right out" that he really opens his heart and gives freely of his own strength.

In his relationship with Melinda, Will gains release from self; his convictions have been proven, and therefore strengthened. Heretofore he has observed and pondered the complexities of human needs; now he has filled one of those needs, and has himself grown and been enriched by actual experience.

In the playing he must illustrate the force of a direct mind, by playing with great honesty and simplicity. He is serious without being solemn, aware without appearing over-sensitive, tender but never maudlin. Brooks Atkinson gave a most valuable clue to the interpretation of the role in his review of the first production. Referring to Mr. Morse's performance as Will, he wrote: "Richard Morse . . . gives an honest, straightforward performance; he does not patronize the part by dwelling on its innocence."

Mrs. Henderson

To Mrs. Henderson the present does not exist. She lives in the past and in the future, in a world as unreal and destroying as that of Mrs. Grant. When Will is expelled from school, she comes up against the present with such force that she is shocked into taking a somewhat realistic view of the fantasies that have been so strenuous to maintain. The weariness that overcomes her then is in sudden contrast to the aggressive strength that she has previously displayed. It is as though she has spent herself, and we can assume that she will henceforth exert less pressure on Will. Having finally faced disillusionment, she has surmounted the greatest hurdle of her life, and nothing can be as bad again.

No attempt need be made by the actress playing Mrs. Henderson to create neuroticism. In fact, she should play against the neurosis, striving for normalcy, which will bring out the humor in the role, and create real sympathy when Mrs. Henderson, with great simplicity and control, takes a clear look into the void that surrounds her.

Mr. Henderson

Mr. Henderson's outer aggression is an armour which he has developed to protect a spirit that is compassionate, courageous, and bewildered. He moves from town to town in a blind groping search for the dignity that life has denied him—accomplishment, friendship, peace.

He does not understand why he is a failure, why his wife hates him. She married him because, in her need for love, she sensed the kindness that was in him. But she needed more than kindness, and he had nothing more to give. He has borne the burden of defeat with a kind of dumb fortitude and a determined lack of self-pity. His moments of lusty rebellion reflect surprise, like the cry of a trapped animal, rather than complaint. His energetic courage in the face of total bafflement has been Will's mainstay, and his unknowing kindness a far more certain form of love than Mrs. Henderson's smothering possessiveness.

Miss Robson

Miss Robson is intended to illustrate the abysmal futility of a desire to help which lacks the knowledge of how to help. She is a behaviorist, a practitioner of applied psychology, and she is pathetic because her striving toward humanity will never do more than scratch the surface, leaving her bewildered and rejected.

She is like someone groping with closed eyes and heavy blundering steps in the right direction, but accomplishing as little, or less, than if she were to stand absolutely still and take a good look around.

Polly

Polly is the personification of success. She has ease and poise, good looks, and the outer confidence of the born leader. For reasons that we will later discover, she has developed a watchful maliciousness, but it is at all times cloaked with an air of smooth good nature and politeness, which reflect the mannerly home in which she has been raised.

We sense the avarice in Polly, so that when she turns on Melinda we are not surprised at the act itself; but she has so convinced us of her security that we *are* surprised at the reasons for the act. We will realize the more forcefully the personal torments that lie beneath many a façade of worldly success.

Bruce

Bruce is a nice boy, a handsome, rather unthinking egotist, in whom there are vague strivings of gentleness and love. He has been swept along on the tide of social condemnation of Melinda, but when he gets a closer glimpse of her, during rehearsals of the play, his eyes become cleared for a moment and his better instincts struggle from their hiding place. But they are weak, and at the first word of accusation against Melinda they desert him. When he turns on her, the words are cruel, but the manner of delivery carries with it a sense of hurt, and a deep shame at what he is doing.

Anne and Eleanor

Anne and Eleanor are all the people who follow in the shadow of the "Privileged," admiring and emulating the Popular One who seems to have no fears or insecurities. Polly stands to them as a goddess, whose nod of approval is a sign of hope that they too may one day achieve perfect happiness.

Polly's frantic clutching at her crumbling prestige is surely based on a deep sense that if the girls were to witness her humiliation they would promptly detach themselves from her in sorrow and disillusionment and seek another idol. And so they would.

Teach Me How to Cry

ACT I

Scene 1

The Grant living room, D. S. L.
Mrs. Grant is seated on sofa, sewing. She looks young, calm. Hair and dress youthful. Tea tray is set on table or tea rack before her. After a moment, Miss Robson appears from L., approaches door from outside, rings doorbell. Mrs. Grant starts, looks up, frightened. Slowly puts down sewing. To hall, suspicious, looks furtively out window. At mirror, slowly smooths her hair, straightens dress. Faces door, takes a deep breath. Opens door.

MISS ROBSON. (*After slight pause. Mrs. Grant is staring at her.*) Good afternoon. You must be Melinda's mother!
MRS. GRANT. Yes.
MISS ROBSON. (*Smiles.*) I'm Miss Robson. Jane Robson.
MRS. GRANT. Jane?
MISS ROBSON. Robson. I teach Melinda at school.
MRS. GRANT. Melinda's teacher!
MISS ROBSON. Yes, Mrs. Grant. I'm delighted to meet you at last. May I come in?
MRS. GRANT. Come in? Oh, please come in. (*Miss Robson enters. Mrs. Grant closes door, leads the way into living room. Very happy.*) Melinda's teacher. Oh, your coat. I'll take it and— will I take it, or ——
MISS ROBSON. Oh, it's just an old coat. I'll toss it over a chair. (*Puts it over arm of chair R.*)
MRS. GRANT. Sit down. Take that chair—or would you rather sit here? That's comfortable, but this is an antique. (*As she indicates sofa.*)
MISS ROBSON. This will be just dandy. (*Sits on chair R.*)
MRS. GRANT. (*Goes C. to sofa, sits.*) Oh, I'm so glad you came. (*Indicates tea rack.*) You see, I have tea made and everything.

MISS ROBSON. How very nice!
MRS. GRANT. (*Pouring.*) Yes, it's nice. I make it every day at four o'clock, and drink it all by myself. (*Smiles.*) I put out an extra cup—always—in case I have a visitor. And now I have. I wish I could have looked forward to it. Do you take milk and sugar?
MISS ROBSON. A little milk, if you please.
MRS. GRANT. A little milk. (*Adds it carefully.*) Isn't it a perfectly lovely day! Did you come through the park on your way? (*Takes tea over to her.*)
MISS ROBSON. No, I didn't waste time. I came straight from school. (*Takes tea.*) Thank you. (*Mrs. Grant is standing over her, watching her anxiously. She smiles a little nervously and sips tea.*)
MRS. GRANT. Is it all right?
MISS ROBSON. It's just grand! I'll tell you why I came, Mrs. Grant.
MRS. GRANT. (*Disappointed.*) Didn't you come to see me?
MISS ROBSON. Indeed I did. And at the same time, I thought we might have a little chat about Melinda.
MRS. GRANT. (*A little alarm.*) She is a good girl, isn't she?
MISS ROBSON. Oh, extremely good. But perhaps—not entirely happy.
MRS. GRANT. Oh, she's very happy! We're always happy together. (*Pleased.*) I make her beautiful clothes. Dresses—all different and lovely. Silk, every single one of them. So she'll be nicer than anyone in school. And she does look nice, doesn't she? In her pretty dresses?
MISS ROBSON. I'm sure you *make* the dresses, Mrs. Grant. I've seen much of your lovely work. I had a very dear friend who was married in a dress you made.
MRS. GRANT. Oh . . . (*She sits on sofa, pours tea for herself.*)
MISS ROBSON. But you know that Melinda always wears plain skirts and blouses to school.
MRS. GRANT. (*A little frown.*) I tell her to wear the dresses. Maybe you would tell her to wear the dresses.
MISS ROBSON. She always looks neat and nice. It's what goes on inside her I'm concerned about.
MRS. GRANT. When you came through the park—I wonder if the cherry trees are in bloom?
MISS ROBSON. I—I believe they are. But I didn't ——

MRS. GRANT. I must walk over and look at them then. One day when the sun is shining. I was watching the sun today, out the window. The world looked beautiful. There was no one on the street. Just the sun. It was noon, and there were no shadows.
MISS ROBSON. Yes—you live on a lovely quiet street.
MRS. GRANT. It isn't—always quiet. People knock on the door. Ring the bell. Men, sometimes. The milkman—Melinda pays him, when she's here. Once a man wanted inside to fix the telephone. (*Frowns.*) That was what he said. To fix the telephone. I never use the telephone.
MISS ROBSON. I suppose Melinda does though. Young girls—at that age. (*She smiles.*)
MRS. GRANT. No, not much. You phoned her once, didn't you?
MISS ROBSON. Yes.
MRS. GRANT. You talk to her—because you like her.
MISS ROBSON. And I like to think I can help her.
MRS. GRANT. You do help her. She gets high marks.
MISS ROBSON. She's very intelligent. She's far advanced intellectually. But—emotionally ——
MRS. GRANT. (*Firmly.*) Melinda is never emotional.
MISS ROBSON. No ——
MRS. GRANT. Never. We have pleasant times together, just the two of us . . . we talk. About everything that's nice. I hope you talk to her about nice things.
MISS ROBSON. Oh, indeed I do. Now there's the choir, for instance. Melinda says she can't sing—but that's only an evasion.
MRS. GRANT. She sings for me. Lullabies.
MISS ROBSON. She needs to sing at school, Mrs. Grant.
MRS. GRANT. She can sing at school.
MISS ROBSON. But she doesn't. She doesn't join in anything. It's as though she's—afraid.
MRS. GRANT. Those cherry trees, when they were planted long ago, I said a prayer that they would grow happy and nothing would beat them down.
MISS ROBSON. Have you—always lived in this town, Mrs. Grant?
MRS. GRANT. Always? I—I was born here—and I've been here—in this house. (*Looks toward window.*) It's clouding over.
MISS ROBSON. (*Rises, goes to sofa.*) Melinda may be home soon, Mrs. Grant. I can explain very quickly how you and I can

help her. (*As she speaks, she reaches out to put her cup and saucer down on tea rack and sits on sofa. Mrs. Grant thinks Miss Robson is offering the cup to her, and reaches for it. A second's hesitation, and Miss Robson gives it to her. Mrs. Grant balances the tea cup and saucer in one hand, and her own in the other, looking at them in panic. Her hands tremble . . . she cannot cope with the two tea cups. How can she cope with Miss Robson? She manages to get both cups set down on rack. Almost simultaneously she rises, overcome with fear.*)

MRS. GRANT. (*Rises.*) Why do you tell me to help her? I do help her. I look after her.

MISS ROBSON. You needn't be frightened, Mrs. Grant.

MRS. GRANT. I'm not. (*Turns. Stands looking out window.*)

MISS ROBSON. (*Shaken but undaunted.*) You see, it's only about the play. The senior class play—Romeo and Juliet. I would like Melinda to try out for the role of Juliet. It's a pity you won't allow her to take part, Mrs. Grant. Now, if it's her studies you're concerned about——

MRS. GRANT. (*Turns.*) I won't allow her? I won't—but I didn't know. She didn't tell me there was going to be a play.

MISS ROBSON. (*Surprised.*) Didn't she?

MRS. GRANT. Melinda loves to play-act. When she was a little girl, we used to play together. (*Looks at dolls.*) We played with the dolls. (*Defiantly, as though someone might take them away from her.*) They're my dolls, from when I was a little girl, and Melinda and I played house together. Now she won't play with them any more, although I plead with her. I make beautiful clothes for them . . . lovely silk dresses. (*Pleased.*) I'll make her costumes for the play!

MISS ROBSON. Then you consent to her being in the play?

MRS. GRANT. I'll make all her costumes. Won't she need a lot of pretty dresses?

MISS ROBSON. Yes——

MRS. GRANT. (*Sits on sofa again.*) Oh, I'm so glad you came. May I pour you some more tea?

MISS ROBSON. Yes, thank you. Do you think you could encourage her, Mrs. Grant? It would be an important step for her. Melinda reads exquisitely in English class. And so I'm sure she would be a great success, which would in turn give her confidence.

I'm convinced—if she can gain in confidence, she will then begin facing up to life. She won't make friends as long as she runs away.
MRS. GRANT. (*Has been pouring tea. Now she stops.*) Melinda has lots of friends.
MISS ROBSON. (*A slight pause. Kindly, but firmly.*) She has no friends at all, Mrs. Grant. Not one. Melinda is terribly lonely.
MRS. GRANT. (*Stands.*) How can she be lonely? Everyone likes her. I'm her mother and I know! You're only her teacher. I teach her more things than you do! (*She exits, still carrying cup and saucer. Goes to front hall, stands just outside the doorway. She sets the cup and saucer down on table, looks in mirror, slowly smooths her hair. In the living room, Miss Robson is puzzled. Rises, takes a step toward door.*)
MISS ROBSON. Mrs. Grant . . . (*Instantaneously, with the smooth ease of a shadow, Mrs. Grant moves away from the doorway, just a few steps down the hall, where she is still visible to us but not to Miss Robson. Miss Robson slowly crosses to window, R., stands looking out. Melinda enters, from outside, closes door. She is sixteen. She holds herself completely in check.*)
MRS. GRANT. (*With relief.*) Oh, Melinda. (*Melinda kisses her mother. Turns and puts school books on table.*) I'm so glad you're home, sweetheart. I was waiting for you.
MELINDA. Yes, Mother. (*Stands facing her mother, waiting quietly.*)
MRS. GRANT. How was school?
MELINDA. Fine.
MRS. GRANT. Oh, I forgot! We have a visitor!
MELINDA. —Visitor?
MRS. GRANT. (*Pleased.*) She came for tea. You'll be pleased—come, sweetheart. (*She takes Melinda into the living room. Melinda stops just inside doorway, stares at Miss Robson, who rises. Mrs. Grant gets Miss Robson's tea cup from the hall.*)
MISS ROBSON. (*Has pulled herself together and is her reliable cheery self.*) Hello there, Melinda. (*Melinda just stares.*)
MRS. GRANT. It's your teacher, Melinda.
MELINDA. How do you do, Miss Robson.
MISS ROBSON. It's such a grand day for a walk—I thought I'd just pop over and introduce myself to your mother. (*She sits on chair R.*)

MRS. GRANT. (*Contentedly, handing tea cup to Miss Robson.*) We've been having tea together. (*Goes to sofa, sits.*)
MELINDA. (*Sits on sofa, placing herself between her mother and the chair on which Miss Robson is seated.*) Did you sew something nice today, Mother?
MRS. GRANT. Oh, yes.
MELINDA. May I see it? (*To Miss Robson.*) My mother sews— she makes beautiful things. She's very clever.
MISS ROBSON. I know she is, dear.
MELINDA. She shows me when I get home. It's always something wonderful, and I'm proud of her. (*Mrs. Grant hands her sewing. . . . Melinda takes it, barely glances at it. To Miss Robson:*) And then we have tea together, every afternoon, just the two of us.
MRS. GRANT. But, Melinda. You don't ——
MELINDA. My mother puts out an extra cup—that's for me.
MISS ROBSON. (*Holds up her cup.*) Then I had yours today.
MRS. GRANT. No. Because Melinda doesn't ——
MELINDA. May I have some tea please, Mother? Would you— would you mind getting me a cup?
MRS. GRANT. (*Stands.*) Of course, sweetheart. (*She exits, going L. from the hall into the wings.*)
MISS ROBSON. (*After a slight hesitation.*) Melinda ——
MELINDA. I didn't know you were coming to see my mother.
MISS ROBSON. She's very, very nice, dear.
MELINDA. Did I do anything wrong in school?
MISS ROBSON. Of course not.
MELINDA. I came straight home.—I don't understand ——
MISS ROBSON. Well, you see, I didn't have a class last period.
MELINDA. Then you've been here for half an hour.
MISS ROBSON. Oh, Melinda—you mustn't worry ——
MELINDA. No, I'm not worried.
MRS. GRANT. (*Enters with cup and saucer.*) Now we can have a tea party all together. (*Sits, pours tea, hands cup to Melinda.*)
MISS ROBSON. (*Drinks tea.*) Melinda told you of the wonderful mark she got in English composition, I suppose, Mrs. Grant.
MRS. GRANT. I suppose ——
MISS ROBSON. I spend many of my afternoons visiting the parents of my pupils, but I can't always be so sincere in my praise.
MRS. GRANT. Do you ask them all to be in the play? (*Melinda*

puts down her tea on rack. Glances at her mother, then at Miss Robson.)
MISS ROBSON. Indeed I don't.
MELINDA. (*To Miss Robson.*) But we decided about the play.
MISS ROBSON. I thought perhaps, dear, you hadn't—really decided——
MELINDA. But I have. I've decided.
MRS. GRANT. You've decided to be in it?
MELINDA. No. (*To Miss Robson.*) Is that what you came to talk about?
MRS. GRANT. (*Disappointed.*) Melinda, aren't you going to be in the play?
MELINDA. No! You wouldn't want me to! You'd be lonely.
MRS. GRANT. (*To Miss Robson. Helplessly.*) I don't know. It's whatever Melinda wants. Whatever would be nice for her.
MISS ROBSON. (*To Melinda.*) It—would be nice for you——
MRS. GRANT. It would be *very* nice for you.
MELINDA. It wouldn't! I'd hate it!
MRS. GRANT. (*Low.*) You mustn't say that word—ever!
MELINDA. (*To Miss Robson.*) It isn't that I'd hate it——
MRS. GRANT. (*Stands.*) You've said it again. (*Leaves, goes to hall. Stands there, still. Melinda watches her mother leave. Mute.*)
MISS ROBSON. I'm terribly sorry if I've upset your mother, Melinda.
MELINDA. (*Holding her head high.*) She isn't upset. My mother likes to go out of the room sometimes.
MISS ROBSON. (*Stands and crosses to sofa.*) Has she gone -——
MELINDA. (*Stands.*) She hasn't gone anywhere. Just away. (*Goes R. to doll rack.*) Have you seen my dolls? (*Stands looking at dolls, without touching them, her back to Miss Robson.*)
MISS ROBSON. Melinda. (*Crosses to her.*) Now I want you to compose yourself, dear, and listen to me. (*Melinda takes a doll up into her arms.*) It's only a play, after all, and there's no need to take it very seriously one way or the other. Are you listening, Melinda?
MELINDA. (*Turns and faces her, holding doll.*) Yes, Miss Robson.
MISS ROBSON. Good. Which doll is that, dear? What's her name?
MELINDA. She hasn't got a name. She's nobody.

MISS ROBSON. (*With an enthusiastic smile . . . completely uncomprehending.*) I see!
MELINDA. (*Crosses L.*) Dolls don't deserve names.
MISS ROBSON. (*Follows her.*) Melinda, if you will just tell me why you don't want to be in the play, then I'm sure we can have a little talk and straighten it out.
MELINDA. It's on account of my name. I think people would—they'd read the program, and they'd think Juliet shouldn't be played by someone strange called Melinda.
MISS ROBSON. (*Dismissing this foolishness.*) Now, Melinda! You know what a good time they have at rehearsals. And there's the dance this Friday night, to begin the Fund Raising. Had you thought about going?
MELINDA. Yes, I thought about it.
MISS ROBSON. (*Chummy.*) Well, why don't you go with me? And you can wear a party dress if you want to. I'm sure you have a pretty dress. (*She starts to put her arm around Melinda's shoulder. At her touch, Melinda stiffens and stands back.*)
MELINDA. I—I have something else I have to do on Friday night. Thank you anyway.
MISS ROBSON. Oh. (*For an instant she is defeated.*) Well . . . (*Looks to window.*) It does seem to have clouded over badly, doesn't it? I suppose—if I don't want to get caught in the rain —— (*She heads for her coat.*)
MELINDA. Don't you like rain?
MISS ROBSON. Heavens, no. I wish you'd think about the dance, dear.
MELINDA. (*Politely.*) Yes, Miss Robson.
MISS ROBSON. Now then—I should say good-bye to your mother.
MELINDA. She's in the hall. Mother! (*Melinda leads the way to hall. Miss Robson follows.*)
MISS ROBSON. (*In the doorway.*) Ah! (*Reaches out to shake hands, but changes her mind as Mrs. Grant does not respond.*) Thank you for the lovely tea, Mrs. Grant. (*To Melinda.*) And you'll think over what I said, won't you, dear?
MELINDA. Yes, Miss Robson.
MISS ROBSON. Just remember. Nothing ventured, nothing gained. Good-bye. (*She exits.*)
MRS. GRANT. (*Very shaken.*) Close the door, Melinda. (*Melinda*

closes door slowly. *Turns to mother.*) You're playing with the doll! (*Melinda shakes her head. Goes to living room. Mrs. Grant follows.*) Aren't you playing with the doll, Melinda?
MELINDA. I was only showing it to Miss Robson.
MRS. GRANT. She has her best dress on.
MELINDA. It isn't a she. It's only a doll. (*Wearily, hands the doll carelessly to her mother.*)
MRS. GRANT. (*Reproachfully, accusingly.*) You always wear those blouses and skirts to school. I make you pretty clothes. Your hair—I wish you'd comb your hair sometimes, Melinda. People won't think I take care of you. And I do. (*With tenderness she replaces the doll on rack.*) A good mother takes care of her children.
MELINDA. Mother. When Miss Robson was here—before I got home—did anything happen?
MRS. GRANT. We had tea, and everything was nice. (*To sofa. Sits. She has begun to recover.*)
MELINDA. (*Intensely, pleading.*) Please, I want to know.
MRS. GRANT. But it's nicer now that we're alone. That's always the best. (*Picks up sewing.*) Now tell me about today, sweetheart.
MELINDA. (*To sofa. Sits. Dutifully.*) Everything was fine. (*Mrs. Grant smiles, sews.*) The teachers were nice to me, and smiled. And then—after school—I walked home with Polly and the girls. And—we talked, and had a good time.
MRS. GRANT. What do you talk about?
MELINDA. Polly talks about Bruce. (*A touch of warmth.*) Bruce is the nicest boy in the whole school and everybody likes him, but he likes Polly best. Everybody likes her best.
MRS. GRANT. She's your best friend, isn't she? Isn't she, Melinda?
MELINDA. There's a new boy at school. His name is Will, and he's terrible.
MRS. GRANT. Then we won't talk about him.
MELINDA. He wasn't paying attention during geometry and Mr. Bremner asked him what he was thinking about. He said, a poem that he was writing. In his head. And then Mr. Bremner said for him to stand up and say it out loud to everybody and get it out of his head so there'd be room for geometry. And so he did. He wasn't afraid or anything. He's terrible.
MRS. GRANT. I had a visitor today. Old Miss Willer. She's kind

and lovely, and she came to see me this morning. Not to order a dress or anything, but just to see me. She had a letter. It was a letter from a friend, and she gave it to me. Miss Willer's friend lives away off in California, and she writes letters and Miss Willer gives them to me when she's through. At the end of them it says, "Love." And I had another visitor. Two in one day. Your teacher —— (*To Melinda. Bewildered.*) It was about you. I hope you've been a good girl at school, Melinda.

MELINDA. Yes, I have, Mother.

MRS. GRANT You must always be a good girl, Melinda. You'll remember that, won't you?

MELINDA. Yes.

MRS. GRANT. Remember to be good.

MELINDA. (*A pause. Then, pleading.*) Mother. What is good? What does it mean?

MRS. GRANT. What does it mean? (*They stare at each other. From outside, a low rumble of thunder. Mrs. Grant stands.*) It's going to rain. (*Melinda looks toward window. Stands. Starts slowly toward window. Mrs. Grant hurries past her to window.*) You're not to go out in the rain, Melinda! You always go out in the rain! The thing to do when it rains is to close the curtains. (*Pulls curtains closed. Turns to Melinda. Smiles.*) Now we can pretend the sun is shining.

MELINDA. But it isn't, it isn't!

MRS. GRANT. Your teacher said something else. Sweetheart, you're going to be in a play. That will be lovely ——

MELINDA. I'm not going to be in it.

MRS. GRANT. Melinda, please!

MELINDA. There's everything else too. A dance—the dance is on Friday. I'd have to go to it.

MRS. GRANT. (*Eagerly.*) You could wear the party dress. I made it so carefully for you, and you never did wear it, not even once. Won't you try it on and see how pretty you look?

MELINDA. I couldn't ——

MRS. GRANT. (*Stamps her foot suddenly with shrill petulant anger.*) *You* could! I'll help you! I'll get the dress, and help you put it on. You'll see how pretty you look! (*She exits.*)

MELINDA. (*Following across room.*) I couldn't — please don't —— (*Stops near door, looks around room frantically. Sees dolls, goes to them.*) I hate you. I hate you. (*A clap of thunder*

and the rain starts suddenly. She listens to the rain. Relaxes. Turns and walks to window. Opens curtains and stands looking out. Mrs. Grant returns carrying white party dress.)
MRS. GRANT. I brought the dress, Melinda. *(No answer. She holds up dress, looks at it, smiles.)* It's pretty, like a wedding dress. *(Puts it carefully over chair.)* I like to look at it. It looks clean and good. *(She goes to sofa, sits, looking at dress. In a dream.)*
MELINDA. *(Turns slowly.)* Mother, were you ever in a play?
MRS. GRANT. Perhaps I was.
MELINDA. Was it—did you like it?
MRS. GRANT. I like everything that ever happened.
MELINDA. *(Tense.)* But I mean really? *(Rushes over to her.)* You wouldn't think about yourself, would you, because you'd be someone else. Either you're—yourself—or someone else. That's easy to understand. You have to be *somebody!*
MRS. GRANT. *(Giggles a little. Not in any way a silly or crazy giggle, but charming and young . . . the sweet way two little girls giggle together.)* Somebody! Of course you have to be somebody.
MELINDA. *(Breathlessly . . . goes down on her knees by her mother.)* Yes . . . today in school we did a drawing. A tree . . . a family tree. Mine had blossoms on it, and pretty colors. *(Slight pause.)* Then we put on the people.
MRS. GRANT. What people?
MELINDA. The ones in our family. Our—relatives. Polly put on her father—that's the doctor. And her mother. And then her grandparents. *(Mrs. Grant sews.)* What's my grandmother's name? I have to know the name—to put on the tree.
MRS. GRANT. Trees don't have people!
MELINDA. It's only make believe!
MRS. GRANT. If you want to make believe, you should be in the play.
MELINDA. I want to be in it!
MRS. GRANT. Then why don't you be?
MELINDA. *(Slowly stands.)* I'm afraid.
MRS. GRANT. Did I show you my sewing? It's a wedding dress for Miss Allison to get married in.
MELINDA. It's nice! *(She looks down at her mother, barely breathing.)* Was your wedding dress nice, Mother?

MRS. GRANT. My wedding dress?
MELINDA. What was it like?
MRS. GRANT. (*Looks front.*) My wedding dress was —— Miss Allison's dress is white.
MELINDA. Was your wedding dress white?
MRS. GRANT. I never had a white dress. I make you white dresses, but I never did have a white dress. I had a blue dress once. There was a band playing.
MELINDA. (*A pause. Walks to chair, looks down at dress.*) In the play, I could be Juliet. And I could put her parents on my tree. (*Slowly takes up dress. Holds it to her.*)
MRS. GRANT. (*Smiles at her.*) That looks nice, sweetheart.
MELINDA. (*Slowly she takes a few steps downstage. She is speaking to herself and the universe, but excluding her mother.*) I'm going to wear it to the dance. Juliet went to a dance . . . and she wasn't afraid!

BLACKOUT

ACT I

Scene 2

After a brief pause, we hear a blast of gay young dance music. Lights then come up on Section D. S. C. *It is the night of the dance, and it will soon be established that this is intended to be a terrace leading from the High School Gymnasium.*
After a few seconds, Polly and Bruce come dancing from behind the Henderson Set at R., *and make their entrance* C. *Bruce is swinging Polly gayly and vigorously. She wears a party dress, as do all the girls. The music comes to an end when this number is finished, and does not begin again until the end of the scene.*

POLLY. (*Breaks away from him, out of breath and laughing.*) Bruce, you're terrible!
BRUCE. What did I do?
POLLY. You dance with me as if you own me!

BRUCE. If I owned you, I wouldn't dance with you at all. (*Grins.*) I'd take you to the bandstand.
POLLY. Oh, the things you say!
BRUCE. (*Teasing.*) It'd be nice up there on the bandstand, Polly. (*Goes to her, puts an arm around her, points upward.*) Look at that moon. (*They both look up.*)
POLLY. It's pretty . . .
BRUCE. We'd be closer to it up there.
POLLY. (*Smiles.*) We're close enough right here on the terrace. (*She breaks away and twirls around.*) Oh, what a heavenly night. Do you suppose it's true about Hilda?
BRUCE. What about her?
POLLY. They say she went up to the bandstand with Sam King. Sam hinted to Howie . . .
BRUCE. Well, if it is true, Sam oughta shut up about it.
POLLY. (*Laughs.*) Oh, you're being so noble, getting in practice to play Romeo.
BRUCE. (*Gaily.*) That's a good idea! (*He starts over to her.*) Let's practice some of the love scenes.
POLLY. (*Holds out her hands, stopping him. Smiles.*) I can't do that. I haven't got the part yet.
BRUCE. Well, you're going to, aren't you? You always play the leads.
POLLY. I started memorizing the part and everything. But then Mr. Chesley decided to hold auditions. I don't think it's fair. I mean, people are going to be disappointed, that's all.
BRUCE. Aw, you'll win. I'll put in a word for you. (*Melinda enters from behind living room set* L., *walks slowly to* C. *and enters.*)
POLLY. (*Pleasantly.*) Hello, Melinda.
MELINDA. Hello.
BRUCE. Well, Melinda, you're looking mighty pretty. Where've you been all my life? (*Melinda glances at him uncertainly.*)
POLLY. (*Walks past Bruce, stung at his interest in Melinda.*) That dress really looks quite nice on you . . . honestly it does. Are you having a good time?
MELINDA. Yes, thank you.
POLLY. That's nice. Who did you come with?
MELINDA. I came by myself.

POLLY. Oh, that's a shame. You haven't seen that awful Will Henderson around, have you?
MELINDA. No.
POLLY. (*Friendly.*) He's a terrible pest. He's been chasing me all evening. (*Turns to Bruce.*) If you see him, I wish you'd tell him to stop being so fresh. (*Melinda sits on bench at* L.)
BRUCE. Tell you what I'll do. I'll challenge him to a duel. (*To Melinda.*) I have to get in practice anyway. (*He strikes a fencing attitude, showing off for both of them.*) Show you how it goes. (*He dances around.*) It all depends on footwork. You concentrate on the feet and the sword takes care of itself. (*Melinda watches him furtively, admiringly.*)
POLLY. (*Bored with his antics.*) Bruce, I'm hungry. Let's go and get something to eat.
BRUCE. Stay where you are, my beauty. I shall bring a morsel in a gilded goblet. But firstly, I must do in this deadly adversary. (*Again turns on his foe with a fierce roar.*) Ahhhh! Back up, you scum! (*Fights his way up to entrance and through it. He pauses, bows, doffing an imaginary hat as he nearly collides with Anne and Eleanor who have entered from* R. *behind Henderson set.*) Pardon me, ladies, a thousand pardons. (*Girls giggle. He exits and goes* L. *Enter Anne and Eleanor. They see Polly. They go to her.*)
ANNE. Polly, we've been looking all over.
ELEANOR. Have you heard about Hilda?
POLLY. (*Sits on bench* R., *pats bench on either side for them to sit, and they do. All three huddle together cosily.*) Is there anything new?
ANNE. Someone saw her up at the bandstand with a boy!
POLLY. Good heavens, I know all about that. So what?
ELEANOR. So what! Well, you know what it means.
ANNE. (*Sees Melinda.*) Shhh. You'd better not talk about—— (*Anne nudges Eleanor . . . indicates Melinda who is sitting stiffly, her back half turned to them. They all throw her a brief glance and then ignore her.*)
POLLY. Any girl that goes to that place deserves exactly what she gets.
ANNE. Maybe she didn't DO anything.
POLLY. When a place has a reputation like that, you don't have to do anything.
ANNE. She'll probably be expelled.

POLLY. No, she won't. Miss Robson will have a "talk" with her. She had a talk with me once. I could hardly keep a straight face.
ELEANOR. What did she talk about?
POLLY. I can't even remember. A person has to simply tolerate her talks because they're her release.
ANNE. Her what?
POLLY. Release. For her frustration. Because she's so frustrated.
ANNE. Oh, Polly, the things you say!
POLLY. My father's a doctor, isn't he? He knows about these things. Everybody's frustrated. Look at Juliet.
ELEANOR. But, Polly, she killed herself.
POLLY. (*Airily.*) And there you are!
ANNE. (*Impressed.*) You're awfully clever, Polly.
ELEANOR. Come on, we'd better get back. The boys are waiting. (*She rises, starts up* C. *and sees Will Henderson wandering on from* R. *She comes back down.*) Here comes that Will Henderson.
ANNE. (*To Polly.*) Really? He's been looking for you.
ELEANOR. (*Thrilled.*) He's kind of cute.
POLLY. Eleanor, go and find Bruce. He'll be at the refreshment table. Keep him talking for a while.
ELEANOR. What'll I talk to him about?
POLLY. Something he's fascinated with! Bruce! (*Gives Eleanor a shove.*) Go on, get going!
ELEANOR. —All right, Polly. (*They exit* L., *looking curiously at Will Henderson who is entering* R.)
WILL. (*Looks around. Sees Melinda, then Polly. Goes to Polly.*) Say, listen, you promised me a dance.
POLLY. (*Coolly.*) I beg your pardon?
WILL. I said, you promised me a dance. Don't you remember? I asked you when you first got here, and you ——
POLLY. Yes, I remember you asking me. But I don't believe we've been introduced.
WILL. Sure we have. I'm Will Henderson. I'm in your class.
POLLY. (*Aloof . . . leading him on.*) That can hardly be considered an introduction.
WILL. (*A slight pause.*) What's the matter anyway? If you don't want to dance with me, all you've got to do is just say so. Just a straight yes or no.
POLLY. (*A trifle dismayed.*) All right. No.

WILL. (*Defiantly.*) Okay! (*He wanders across stage to Melinda.*) You're Melinda Grant, aren't you?
MELINDA. Yes.
WILL. We're in the same class too.
MELINDA. I know.
WILL. What do you think of a person that promises a person a dance and then won't deliver?
POLLY. (*Stands. Angrily.*) And I'd appreciate not being discussed in public!
WILL. What do you think, Melinda?
MELINDA. I don't see why she should dance with you if she doesn't feel like it.
WILL. But she promised.
MELINDA. Maybe she felt like it then.
POLLY. I didn't. I never felt like dancing with him, and I didn't promise him either. (*Goes to Will.*) I think you're the rudest boy I ever met! You—you have—no finesse whatever! (*With a pretty and furiously indignant toss of her head, she exits and goes off* L.)
WILL. (*Watches her go.*) Girls like that, they make me sick. I despise that type of girl. (*Swinging around to Melinda. Belligerently.*) Is she a friend of yours?
MELINDA. Yes. (*She has risen and started* U. C. *as though to exit. But he blocks the exit, facing her.*)
WILL. Well, I don't like your type of friends!
MELINDA. I don't care whether you do or not. (*Not knowing what to do, she goes back to her bench,* L., *and sits rigidly.*)
WILL. Okay, that makes us even! (*He marches over to bench,* R., *and sits. There is an inner struggle, and then his shoulders sag in despair.*) I do that kind of thing all the time. Antagonize people. You know what I mean? (*Looks over at her. Speaks in amazement.*) I don't mean to antagonize them, I just do. You'd think I did it on purpose, the way I do it, but it isn't on purpose. People are always surprised at me, but they're not as surprised as I am. (*Runs his fingers through his hair in bewilderment. He is struck by a new idea. Gets up, goes over to her, speaks politely.*) Would —would you care to dance with me?
MELINDA. No, thank you.
WILL. (*Slight pause.*) Do you want me to go away?
MELINDA. I don't care.

WILL. Well, if you don't out and out despise me, at least that's something. (*Goes back to his bench, sits.*) I'm new here.
MELINDA. I know.
WILL. I've noticed you though. You're different from the other girls. (*She doesn't answer.*) Are you going to be in this play they're putting on?
MELINDA. I don't know.
WILL. I'm not. (*Pause.*) Do you know why not? (*She just looks at him solemnly.*) I'm more the writer type. My grandfather was a writer. Did you ever live in reflected glory?
MELINDA. No. I don't think so. Did he write plays?
WILL. (*Gloomily.*) No, they're too interesting. He only wrote stuff that was *boring*. (*Matter-of-factly.*) I'm going to be a writer too. . . . My mother's decided. I write poetry. She hates me writing poetry, but she keeps thinking maybe something better will come of it. (*Pause. Cheerfully, speaks front.*) It's terrible poetry. (*Glances at her.*)
MELINDA. Do you like it here?
WILL. Out here on the terrace?
MELINDA. No, I mean in this town.
WILL. I liked the town we were in before better.
MELINDA. Oh.
WILL. You have a nice park here, though, with cherry blossoms.
MELINDA. I love cherry blossoms.
WILL. (*Very warmly and simply.*) They'd look nice in your hair.
MELINDA. (*Startled into conversation.*) We have four churches.
WILL. Have you? I've only been to one.
MELINDA. (*A pause.*) After you get used to this town, you might like it more.
WILL. No, I don't think so. Because by then we'll probably move.
MELINDA. Why will you move?
WILL. Because that's what we do. Do you know how many different places I've lived in? Guess. (*Full of enthusiasm, he goes over to her bench and sits beside her.*)
MELINDA. (*Pulls back a little.*) I couldn't.
WILL. Go on, just guess.
MELINDA. Well—six.
WILL. Seventeen. A different place for every year of my life.
MELINDA. I'd like that.
WILL. No you wouldn't.

MELINDA. Yes, I would. I hate living here!—Oh—I didn't mean I hate it. It's really quite a nice friendly town—and the people are *friendly*. I really like it here quite a lot.
WILL. I think you probably meant what you said in the first place.
MELINDA. What?
WILL. That you hate it.
MELINDA. No, I didn't mean that! I didn't!
WILL. Okay. Listen, why won't you dance with me?
MELINDA. Because I don't care about dancing.
WILL. (*Eagerly.*) Well, that's a coincidence. Because I don't either.
MELINDA. Then why are you so anxious to dance?
WILL. Yeah, I know. That's what I can't figure out. I like to figure things out, and when I can't I get worried. Sometimes—sometimes I get the feeling that if we'd only stay in one place for a while, I could figure out a few more things.
MELINDA. Why do you move so much?
WILL. On account of my father's business. He's a sort of a salesman. My mother calls him a demonstrator, but he's a salesman.
MELINDA. My father used to go around to different towns selling things too.
WILL. That's a coincidence too. Doesn't he any more?
MELINDA. I don't know. He went away a long time ago, before I could remember.
WILL. That's too bad.
MELINDA. I don't mind. I'm used to it. I wouldn't want a father around. (*A little pause.*) He'd be in the way.
WILL. What would he be in the way of?
MELINDA. Well, my mother—my mother and I have very good times together. We talk about things—like her wedding, for instance. When she and my father were married. She tells me about her dress. It was white.
WILL. Wedding dresses are nice white.
MELINDA. And there was a band played at her wedding.
WILL. A band? I never heard of a thing like a band at a wedding.
MELINDA. Well, there was one at hers. Maybe it was the same band that used to play up on the hill. Where the haunted bandstand is.
WILL. Is it haunted?
MELINDA. They say it is.

WILL. Who do they say haunts it?
MELINDA. Why, I don't believe they say. It's got a *terrible* reputation, and nobody respectable goes there.
WILL. Why not?
MELINDA. Because—well, they just don't. I don't know why. It's all burned down, and it's a terrible place. But it didn't used to be. —My mother tells me how it used to be beautiful, and how the people used to walk up the hill together, and listen to the music. People who were in love. Sometimes she cries when she tells me. Oh—I don't mean she cries very much ——
WILL. That's okay. My mother cries too. All mothers cry.
MELINDA. How do you know they do?
WILL. I figured it out.
MELINDA. (*A pause.*) Do—do fathers?
WILL. No, but they'd like to. So it's worse.
MELINDA. (*A pause.*) I'd like it if you'd recite one of your poems for me.
WILL. I might sometime. If you don't think you'd laugh.
MELINDA. No, I don't think I would. I don't laugh very much.
WILL. Why?
MELINDA. I just don't seem to. Do you?
WILL. Not much. I smile though at lots of things. I saw a dog today—he—he was trying to get away from his shadow.
MELINDA. (*Eagerly . . . losing herself.*) I used to try to do that when I was a little girl. I read about Peter Pan—and he lost his shadow—and he lost his mother too.
WILL. Yeah. The Lost Boys.
MELINDA. No, they weren't lost. Their mothers were.
WILL. It's the same thing.
MELINDA. (*A little pause.*) I don't understand that.
WILL. I had to figure it out for a long time before I did. I figure everything out.
MELINDA. Does it come out even?
WILL. Gee, no. But it comes out, that's the main thing.
MELINDA. I like to think everything comes out even.
WILL. It doesn't though, so why think it does?
MELINDA. But if you think it does, and really can believe it, what does it matter if it doesn't?
WILL. It matters a lot. I'll explain it to you ——

MELINDA. (*As though she had been touched by fire, she stands.*) I—I have to go inside.
WILL. Then I'll go in with you and we'll dance.
MELINDA. No!
WILL. Listen, what's the matter with me?
MELINDA. There isn't anything—it's me—(*Her head high . . . defiantly.*) I don't know how to dance.
WILL. (*Starts toward her. Smiling.*) Then I'll teach you.
MELINDA. (*In panic.*) I don't want to be taught! (*A bird in flight, she runs* U. C. *to exit. Just as she is about to go through, the dance music begins offstage with crashing suddenness. She takes a step back . . . turns to him . . . her voice quiet and trembling.*) I don't . . . want . . . to be taught . . . (*With his eyes on hers, he walks toward her slowly. They stand a second facing each other* U. C. *Then with a quiet gesture he raises his right hand, holding it out to her. She is perfectly still, watching him. Then she begins to raise her left hand.*)

QUICK BLACKOUT

ACT I

Scene 3

There is a pause, during which the kitchen table is moved down. Will removes his coat and takes his place at the kitchen table.
Then lights come up on the Henderson kitchen, D. S. R. *Will is seated at the table, at* R., *concentrating on his homework. Books are spread about on the table, which is set with three places. Mrs. Henderson is* U. S., *at stove, her back to audience. She lifts lids from pots, stirs contents, replaces lids. She moves quickly, inefficiently.*

MRS. HENDERSON. I can't keep the stew warm much longer. It's starting to stick. Everything sticks on this stove —— (*No answer. She turns.*) Oh, you're doing your homework. I'm sorry if I interrupted your train of thought, dear.
WILL. That's okay.

MRS. HENDERSON. I'll try to make less noise. This cheap kitchenware makes the worst racket of any we've had. (*Goes to table, looks it over. Moves a few things. Looks at Will.*) It's awful that you have no decent place to do your homework. You shouldn't have to do your homework in the kitchen, and we shouldn't have to eat in the kitchen either.
WILL. (*Looks up.*) I don't care.
MRS. HENDERSON. Well, you *should* care! That's how everyone starts giving up their values, inch by inch, and getting less and less out of life. You keep your values, Will, and don't ever settle for less than you should. You deserve the best, and some day you're going to have the best! (*She strokes the top of his head with a small tender gesture.*)
WILL. (*Huddles over his work.*) The stew smells good.
MRS. HENDERSON. (*Goes back to stove.*) I put a lot of bay leaf in it to try to drown out the smell of garlic from next door. Bay leaf is no kind of weapon against Italians.
WILL. Their kid—Joe—is in our class. He's okay.
MRS. HENDERSON. (*Pained.*) Don't say "kid," Will. And I'm sure there are more attractive words than "okay." You have that lovely book of synonyms. Where is it?
WILL. I don't remember.
MRS. HENDERSON. (*A pause.*) Will, there's something I've been meaning to speak to you about. (*She sits at table, bites her lip, searches his face. Very confidentially.*) You know, dear, the bathroom is no place to read.
WILL. It's not a community one here.
MRS. HENDERSON. (*Invading his soul.*) You go in there and lock the door. You lock it quietly, but I hear you locking it. You don't have to sneak away with your books, Will. I like you to read. A writer has to read a lot, and I understand that. Heaven knows, that's a thing your mother understands. Are you—are you trying to hide your books from your father?
WILL. No.
MRS. HENDERSON. He wouldn't object to them, because he wouldn't understand them.
WILL. It isn't that.
MRS. HENDERSON. (*Insistently.*) Well, what is it? Why do you lock the door?
WILL. (*A slight pause.*) I guess I got in the habit.

MRS. HENDERSON. Well, it's a habit you should try to get out of. Just because we live in boarding houses, we don't have to lose our dignity. (*She rises, with dignity, then rushes to stove.*) Now it's burning. We'll simply have to go ahead and eat. It wouldn't occur to your father to phone—oh, no! (*Will starts to clear away school books. Mrs. Henderson dumps potatoes out in bowl which she takes from shelves* R. *To table. Takes back two plates to stove, serves stew on them.*) Some day you'll have a proper study, with leather furniture and oak panelling. (*Looks into space, holding plate. With a lost little smile.*) And a high, high ceiling. When your children go into the room, it will look to them like a palace. (*To table, puts down plate.*)

WILL. (*Has deposited books on shelves,* D. R. *Now he sits at* R. *of table.*) What would I do in it?

MRS. HENDERSON. Why, you'd write.

WILL. I don't think I could write, just sitting in a room.

MRS. HENDERSON. That's because you've never had a decent room to write in. (*She sits* C. *They begin eating. Mr. Henderson enters* U. R.) Oh, you're home.

MR. HENDERSON. I just ran into Mrs. Donnelly outside. (*Closes door.*) Hi, Will. (*He goes around table, sits* L., *tucks napkin into vest, gets set to eat.*)

WILL. Hello, Dad.

MRS. HENDERSON. I hope you weren't rude to her. I have to put up with her every day. (*Coolly, observing how he has settled in.*) Supper's on the stove.

MR. HENDERSON. (*Without resentment, goes to stove, starts serving stew.*) Trouble with these places, they don't care. Nobody cares about anything any more. I can remember the time they'd change the whole color scheme for you, glad to do it, delighted. Now they're doing you a great big favor even renting you two of their rotten rooms. (*To table, sits.*) The smaller the town, the worse it is. Well, I gave her a piece of my mind. Three days now the toilet's been on the blink ——

MRS. HENDERSON. (*Wincing.*) Ed, not at the table.

MR. HENDERSON. (*Eating heartily.*) There are certain necessities, Dorothy ——

MRS. HENDERSON. Will, pass your dad the potatoes!

MR. HENDERSON. (*An uncritical observation.*) You should cook

'em in the skins, Dorothy. My mother always cooked 'em in the skins. That's where the food value is.
MRS. HENDERSON. Food value isn't everything. There are other values. We lose sight of them ——
MR. HENDERSON. (*As Will hands him potatoes he smiles warmly at his son.*) Thanks. How's school?
WILL. It's okay.
MRS. HENDERSON. Anyway, these places are only a stop gap. When we have our own home and settle down, and something goes wrong with—with the plumbing—we can fix it ourselves. Will can take care of the lawn. The lawn will be Will's job. And I'll take care of the garden myself.—Ed, did you remember the flower box?
MR. HENDERSON. Flower box?
MRS. HENDERSON. You said you'd pick it up today. I spoke to Mrs. Donnelly, and she said she wouldn't mind a bit. It would look nice from outside, she said.
MR. HENDERSON. She cares about the outside all right. Get 'em in here, that's all she cares, and then soak 'em. I—I'll get that box tomorrow, for sure. I was pretty busy today. (*Mrs. Henderson looks down at her plate.*) I said I'll get it, Dorothy. You can count on it. I just got busy today. Things come up—your life isn't your own—not like sitting on your ass in an office. (*Mrs. Henderson puts her fork down with a bang.*) All right. Your behind. But you've gotta understand. A salesman has to keep on the go.
MRS. HENDERSON. You're not a salesman! You're a demonstrator!
MR. HENDERSON. What's the difference? I demonstrate 'em, and then I sell 'em. Sometimes I sell them. I can't for the life of me see why you ——
MRS. HENDERSON. Don't—don't—argue in front of Will!
MR. HENDERSON. What is he, a china doll? Will—tell your mother, once and for all. I'm a salesman. Nothing to be ashamed of in that. Only thing to be ashamed of is I'm a rotten salesman. (*Cheerfully.*) Lousy! (*Eats.*)
WILL. What the heck, Dad. What does it matter?
MR. HENDERSON. Sure, what the heck! (*Looks at him—a warm smile.*) You're a good kid, you know that?
MRS. HENDERSON. There you go—both of you—"kid"— "heck"—"okay." (*She stands up.*) Sometimes, I—I just —— (*She

chokes up, goes up to window, U. C., stands with her back to them.)

MR. HENDERSON. (*Resigned, penitent, he gets up and goes to her. Gently.*) Dorothy. Listen, kid, I'm sorry. I'll get you two flower boxes, and I'll get 'em tomorrow. Ten. All you want.

MRS. HENDERSON. I only want one.

MR. HENDERSON. I'll get you the biggest one in the joint. Store.

MRS. HENDERSON. (*Quietly.*) I only want one that will fit the window.

MR. HENDERSON. I'll measure it tonight. Come on—eat your stew. (*Leads her to table.*) It's swell stew. (*Mrs. Henderson sits. Picks up fork and pushes food around on her plate. He starts a cheerful blast, and she winces.*) Say, what do you suppose happened today? I finally got to see Doctor Fisher. After three visits and a million phone calls. There must be a hell of a lot of sickness in this town. Well, I lined up with the rest of the patients, and in I marched and introduced myself. "Glad to meet you, Doctor," I said, "the name's Henderson. My boy Will goes to school with your girl Polly," I said. "You've probably seen him hanging around the house." (*To Will, deflated.*) Well, he hadn't even heard of you.

WILL. No, I haven't been to her house.

MR. HENDERSON. Why haven't you? She's pretty, isn't she?

WILL. Yes.

MR. HENDERSON. The Fishers are important in this town. Mrs. Fisher's a big wheel in local society. They'd be a nice entrée into a bunch of good homes. Why don't you take Polly to a show some night, Willy? I'll foot you.

MRS. HENDERSON. Don't—call him Willy.

WILL. I hardly even know her, Dad.

MR. HENDERSON. Know any of her friends?

WILL. Not many. I haven't got friendly yet with many of the kids.

MR. HENDERSON. You went to that big dance couple of weeks ago. Whatever came of that? You've hardly been home since.

MRS. HENDERSON. Does something always have to—come of things? Leave him alone, Ed!

MR. HENDERSON. No harm getting friendly with the right people.

MRS. HENDERSON. A man should get by on his own merits. My father always got by on his own merits.

MR. HENDERSON. He had a lot of merits, your father.
MRS. HENDERSON. He was a great and brilliant man.
MR. HENDERSON. Yeah. (*Will puts down his knife and fork. Stands.*)
MRS. HENDERSON. Where are you going, Will?
WILL. No place. I'm just finished.
MRS. HENDERSON. You shouldn't eat so quickly. It isn't polite. (*Will goes to shelves, picks up a book. Starts out of room.*)
MR. HENDERSON. Hold on a minute. (*Will stops.*) It's for your own good, Will. You've gotta learn to speak up—introduce yourself—make friends. They're the most valuable asset a man can have.
MRS. HENDERSON. He has some friends, Ed. He goes places afternoons and in the evening sometimes.
MR. HENDERSON. You're telling me he does. He's never home any more. Where've you been keeping yourself, Will? If you don't know Polly Fisher and you don't know any of her friends, who do you know?
WILL. One of the people I know is a girl called Melinda.
MR. HENDERSON. (*Eating.*) Melinda who? What's her father do?
WILL. Melinda Grant. Her father used to be ——
MRS. HENDERSON. Melinda Grant! Why, she hasn't got any father! That's the girl who —— Mrs. Duskin upstairs told me all about it. There's something the matter with that girl's mother!
MR. HENDERSON. What's the matter with her?
MRS. HENDERSON. Well, for one thing, she's crazy!
MR. HENDERSON. (*Puts down knife and fork.*) She's what? She's crazy!
MRS. HENDERSON. It was a terrible scandal, Mrs. Duskin says. No one's ever forgotten it. It had something to do with a bandstand some place out on the edge of town on a hill or something. (*Will comes slowly toward table, watching her. She is uneasy.*) Well, the whole town used to go there—and this girl's mother, she wasn't married, was seen hanging around there all one spring with a man. Late, sometimes, after the band had gone home. He deserted her, this man, and she went right off her head. And a little while after that the bandstand was burned down. They never knew who did it—but they had their suspicions—they were pretty sure, Mrs. Duskin says. Then she had the baby, and started calling her-

self Mrs. Grant. (*During this, Will has slowly seated himself at the table, and Mr. Henderson has risen.*)
MR. HENDERSON. And that's who Will's been —— (*To Will.*) How much have you been seeing that girl?
WILL. Every day. She's in my class.
MR. HENDERSON. You been seeing her after class?
WILL. Yes.
MR. HENDERSON. Where?
WILL. Around. In the park. We walk ——
MRS. HENDERSON. Did you know about that girl's background?
WILL. (*Stands.*) There isn't anything the matter with Melinda.
MR. HENDERSON. (*Slaps the table. For a moment, the outraged patriarch.*) Like mother, like daughter! What do you expect her to be—normal, like us?
MRS. HENDERSON. (*Nervously.*) Will likes to be broadminded, Ed.
MR. HENDERSON. Oh, he does, does he?
MRS. HENDERSON. (*Rises, comes around the table to Will.*) But what you don't understand, Will, is that it's her entire background. This—this Mrs. Grant herself came from a very sordid family. I heard all about that too. Her mother committed suicide—and her father —— (*She stops, shaking her head.*) He was a terrible person. A drunkard. When a girl has that sort of family behind her, you can just know the kind of person she is!
WILL. (*Desperately.*) I know the kind of person Melinda is.
MRS. HENDERSON. I hope you're not going to be stubborn about it, Will. A boy with a background like yours. Why, your grandfather would simply die!
WILL. He's already *dead.*
MR. HENDERSON. And don't be rude to your mother. We're both very hard on your mother, Will, and the least we can be is polite.
MRS. HENDERSON. No one has to bother being polite. (*To Will.*) All I want is your word that you'll never see that girl again.
WILL. (*A slight pause.*) Okay.
MR. HENDERSON. Do you mean that, son?
MRS. HENDERSON. He gave his word, Ed, and that means he's on his honor. Will comes from an honorable family. Will, dear, it's for your own good, you realize that, don't you? Your father and I are only interested in giving you proper help and guidance. We

wouldn't be doing our duty as parents if we didn't. You understand, don't you, Will? (*She has been tangling her arms around him . . . yearningly, desperately.*)
WILL. (*Breaks away from her fiercely.*) Sure. I understand. (*He makes a rapid exit,* U. R.)
MR. HENDERSON. (*Watches him go. Goes wearily to table, sits.*) Sometimes I wonder what goes on inside that kid. Sometimes I just can't figure him. Pass the butter.
MRS. HENDERSON. (*Hands it to him.*) It's the kind of life he has to lead. One place after another. (*She sinks down into her chair in discouragement.*)
MR. HENDERSON. Why does he always have to pick such queer companions? Every town has its nuts, and trust Will to find 'em. You remember that moth-eaten old professor he used to visit? Came home and started talking about —— Who the hell was it— some doctor.
MRS. HENDERSON. Freud.
MR. HENDERSON. If he has to get interested in doctors, you'd wonder he wouldn't pick an important one like Doctor Fisher. Take out that girl of his, that Polly. Get in the swing of things.
MRS. HENDERSON. (*Stands. Starts clearing dishes.*) You always expect him to get into the best homes.
MR. HENDERSON. Well, why not? He's got decent manners and I buy him good suits.
MRS. HENDERSON. He'll start meeting the right people when he has a home to invite them to, and not before.
MR. HENDERSON. Is that all friendship means to people these days? The kind of home a boy's got?
MRS. HENDERSON. (*With pathetic longing . . . holding back tears with fierce effort.*) It'll be nice for us too, Ed, when we have a house. I don't think I want brick any more—I've changed my mind. I'd like Spanish stucco in a sunny kind of color. Light yellow. With a portico.
MR. HENDERSON. A what?
MRS. HENDERSON. Portico. It's a kind of porch. It would be so lovely to grow flowers in. I wondered what was depressing me lately, and I decided it was that brick house. It would be much too dark, Ed, and not enough sun for flowers. It's springtime, you see, and that's what got me thinking about it. And there's a lovely

picture—in my new magazine. I'll show you. (*Goes to shelves,* D. R.)
MR. HENDERSON. (*He goes very quiet.*) Dorothy. (*Mrs. Henderson bends down to get magazines.*) Listen—don't.
MRS. HENDERSON. (*Straightens up. Her back to him. Every muscle rigid.*) Don't what?
MR. HENDERSON. (*Heartsick . . . quiet.*) Don't bring out the pictures.
MRS. HENDERSON. (*Turns slowly.*) Do you want your coffee first?
MR. HENDERSON. I don't want—I don't want anything. Isn't there any way—couldn't we manage to be content?
MRS. HENDERSON. Content? Content with what?
MR. HENDERSON. (*Imploringly.*) With what we've got. It isn't much—but it's all we're ever going to have. Dorothy, we're not going to have a house. You—you'd be happier if you could get that through your head. We're not ever going to have a house.
MRS. HENDERSON. (*Walks slowly toward him. In a terrible voice.*) Ed, don't you say that again. (*She brings clenched fists down on table.*) Don't—you—ever—say that again!
MR. HENDERSON. (*Stands. Goes to her, puts a hand on her shoulder.*) Okay, kid. What the heck. Let's see the pictures.

BLACKOUT

ACT I

SCENE 4

After a pause lights come up on the ruins of the bandstand, on raised platform U. S. *Trees, a small bench* R. *The mood is lonely and desolate. The stage is empty.*

WILL'S VOICE. (*After a moment, offstage* R.) Here—this looks like the way.
MELINDA. (*Off* R.) I'm frightened.
WILL. Yeah—this is it all right. (*He emerges from* R., *leading her by the hand. She is carrying a book. He wears a jacket or coat.*)
MELINDA. Will, we shouldn't.

WILL. Shouldn't what?
MELINDA. Come here.
WILL. Why not? It's only a place. (*They walk C., look around.*) An old run down place. I bet there aren't any ghosts at all.
MELINDA. (*Shudders a little.*) It feels as if there are.
WILL. Do many people come here?
MELINDA. No. Hardly anyone. And we shouldn't either. It's a terrible place.
WILL. Listen, I told you what my parents said, didn't I?
MELINDA. Why did they say you can't see me?
WILL. It's just them. It's what they're like. We can't hang around town. So where else is there?
MELINDA. (*Looking around. Softly.*) It's just the way I pictured it.
WILL. How—how did it get burned down?
MELINDA. I don't know.
WILL. (*Watching her.*) Don't you?
MELINDA. People whisper about it—it must have been something terrible—but I don't get to hear things always.
WILL. Did you tell your mother anything about me?
MELINDA. No. (*Looks down at her hands.*)
WILL. (*A step toward her.*) You did, didn't you?
MELINDA. Yes. She—she doesn't like me going out with boys. And you—it's your father —— What's so terrible about being a salesman?
WILL. I don't know. You'd have to ask my mother, she knows all about it. We'll come here, see? Every day. I've got it all figured out.
MELINDA. What will we do?
WILL. (*Goes over to bandstand steps, tests them.*) We'll talk. And just sort of be together.
MELINDA. (*Now she smiles and hugs book to her.*) And you can hear my lines for me.
WILL. Have you got the whole scene memorized?
MELINDA. (*Looks at book.*) I've got the whole play memorized. (*To him.*) But I only need to know the scene for the audition. It's beautiful. The best scene in the play. (*She looks around.*)
WILL. (*Indicates a section of bandstand. Smiles.*) And this could be the balcony.
MELINDA. (*Runs over to it. Up a few steps to a small platform*

section. *Up there, her excitement changes to a feeling of loneliness. She looks down at him.*) I wish you were in the play.
WILL. I'll sit in the front row. Every night! (*He goes to bench, sits back, watching her with assuring admiration.*)
MELINDA. (*Looks front. Fearfully.*) They'll—they'll all be there. Looking at me.
WILL. Sure. And you'll be beautiful. (*A slight pause.*) Melinda.
MELINDA. What?
WILL. I was just saying your name. It has a nice sound. I think Melinda is a pretty name. Prettier even than Juliet.
MELINDA. (*Darkly.*) I don't. I think Melinda is a terrible name.
WILL. A name isn't so very important anyway. I knew a fellow once called Stupanski and the kids used to call him Stoop. Or sometimes Stupid. He wasn't though. He was smart. That was his name, that's all. Melinda—at least Melinda is your own name. Guess where my mother got the idea for my first name from? (*During above speech, he comes over to her, stands on steps, looking up at her.*)
MELINDA. William. (*He points to the book she's holding.*) Oh!
WILL. (*Grins.*) Yeah. If a guy called Shakespeare had come along ever and asked her to marry him, I bet she would've. Then she could have called me Will Shakespeare. She would have liked that.
MELINDA. Are you going to be a poet for a living?
WILL. (*Wanders* R. *across stage.*) No, they don't make any money.
MELINDA. Do you want to make a lot of money?
WILL. No, but my wife will probably want me to.
MELINDA. Why marry her then?
WILL. Because I'll want to, I guess. (*Thunder.*)
MELINDA. It's cloudy. It's going to rain. Do you like rain?
WILL. I don't mind it.
MELINDA. (*With inner intensity.*) I love it. I love it better than anything in the world. I like to be out in it. When it rains in the night, I get up and sit looking at it, and want to go out in the rain.
WILL. (*Watching her.*) I wonder why.
MELINDA. (*Simply.*) Because it's raining. I pretend things. Sometimes that I have a friend walking with me.
WILL. My father says friends are an asset. He's great on friends. Only he hasn't got any. I guess not many people have.
MELINDA. Polly has lots.

WILL. No, she hasn't. She hasn't got one. That's what she's afraid of.
MELINDA. I think my mother had one once. But she lost him.
WILL. That's too bad, to lose a friend.
MELINDA. All the time, when I was a little girl, my mother waited for a letter.
WILL. From her friend?
MELINDA. I think so. She won't let the postman come to our house any more. She thinks it's his fault. And she doesn't want me to write to anyone. But I don't mind. I don't have anyone to write to. (*A little pause.*) Will you be going away?
WILL. Maybe.
MELINDA. You will, won't you? (*He doesn't answer. She goes front and looks down.*) The cliff is steep. I look up at it sometimes when I'm walking home from school. If a person fell down that cliff, they'd be killed.
WILL. I guess they would.
MELINDA. (*Straining forward . . . looking down.*) Or if they were pushed.
WILL. (*A little pause.*) Or if they jumped.
MELINDA. (*Pulls back.*) Sometimes you say terrible things!
WILL. It doesn't hurt to say things, Melinda.
MELINDA. (*Turning on him. Angrily.*) It does! It does!
WILL. Not if they're true.
MELINDA. (*Scornfully.*) What does *true* mean! You don't understand the words you say. Nobody would jump over a cliff.
WILL. Lots of people do. They do it all the time.
MELINDA. *Because they're terrible, terrible cowards, and they don't deserve to live.*
WILL. Now *you're* saying terrible things. Everybody deserves to live.
MELINDA. *I don't.*
WILL. (*Rushes up onto bandstand. Urgently.*) Do you know why you say that? I'll tell you why you say things like that.
MELINDA. I don't want to know!
WILL. You don't want to know anything. So you don't. You don't even know who you are.
MELINDA. Stop talking to me. You talk and talk and I don't understand you.
WILL. (*Suddenly humbled.*) Sure, okay. I'll go away if you want.

MELINDA. Go on then! As far away as you want. (*Will walks to bench.*) I don't know why we came to this terrible place. I hate it here. (*Will sits quietly, watching her. She comes slowly down the steps.*) There aren't any flowers—nothing. There used to be music here. It was springtime, like now, only people used to come here. (*Walks* U. C.)
WILL. We come here.
MELINDA. (*Stands with back to audience.*) They were in love, and they listened to the music. A band played. They were sad. I seem to know it. I seem to hear the music. (*Bring in sound of cornet, muted, playing a sad martial tune. She turns.*) It makes me want to cry.
WILL. Go on then.
MELINDA. No, I never cry.
WILL. You look sometimes as if there are tears behind your eyes.
MELINDA. (*Trembling.*) I'm cold—it's getting cold.
WILL. Come and sit down.
MELINDA. (*Goes to bench and sits beside him. A pause. She is quiet after her outburst.*) Do you really think Melinda is a nice name?
WILL. Yes, I do.
MELINDA. But it isn't as nice as Juliet. If I—if I get the part, then I'll have two whole months to be Juliet.
WILL. You won't be, though.
MELINDA. What?
WILL. It's only pretending for a little while. When the play is over, you'll have to go back to being you.
MELINDA. I wish I didn't.
WILL. (*The light has been fading. Now the rain starts gently. Will looks up.*) It's starting to rain. I'll give you my coat.
MELINDA. No, you don't have to. (*But he gets up and takes off his coat. She looks front, at the rain.*) It's like crying. Like the sky crying.
WILL. (*Putting coat gently over her shoulders.*) The sky knows how to cry. (*He sits. Speaks with simple directness.*) Is your mother insane?
MELINDA. (*A pause. Shocked to her soul.*) That's—a—*terrible*—thing to say. (*The music is out.*)
WILL. I didn't mean anything by it. I only want to know.
MELINDA. Of course she isn't insane!

WILL. What's the matter with her then?
MELINDA. There isn't anything the matter with her! She's—she acts perfectly fine. She's just young. (*Pleading.*) There's nothing wrong with being young!
WILL. There is if you're old.
MELINDA. My mother isn't old!
WILL. Mothers are old. They're old and tired. They get tired after a while.
MELINDA. My mother is never tired! My mother looks after me. She's always there—for me to go home to—and we talk. I can tell her about things—I can ask her things too!
WILL. What things?
MELINDA. Anything! Anything at all! She helps me to understand. She knows about me —— (*Slight pause.*) When you want to know something, you ask your mother. When you're lonely, you go to your mother and she explains things and you're not lonely any more. When you don't understand—when you're frightened in the night—when you're hurt—your mother makes things better. She puts her arms around you, and you can lean on her. You can lean on her. (*She is looking front.*)
WILL. (*Quietly.*) You're crying.
MELINDA. No, I'm not. (*She does not sound as though she's crying.*)
WILL. (*Still watching her.*) Just silently.
MELINDA. It's the rain. (*Will slowly reaches out and touches her cheek.*)
WILL. (*Tastes his finger.*) It's salty. It's tears all right. You don't even cry right out. (*Wonderingly.*) The only way you'd know they were tears is by the taste.
MELINDA. They dry by themselves.
WILL. They're quiet. Tears should bust out—or they're no good. Lean on me. Lean on me, Melinda, and cry right out! (*Melinda remains motionless, staring out front. Will very still, watching her. Pause. Lights dim to BLACKOUT. After an instant, a flash of lightning. They are revealed clearly, and Melinda is in Will's arms, her face buried on his shoulder. Then a slow roll of thunder, followed by a hard crash of thunder. . . .*)

CURTAIN

ACT II

Scene 1

Lights come up on the bandstand. In these weeks, flowers have bloomed, and there are bright patches of green here and there. The sun shines in the late afternoon, casting long shadows. An atmosphere of peace and beauty.
Will is on the bandstand itself, comes slowly down the steps, wanders across stage. He and a bird whistle back and forth at each other. He watches it as it flies across the sky. He is relaxed and happy.

WILL. (*Calls* U. S.) How you coming along?
MELINDA'S VOICE. (*Off* R.) I'm nearly changed.
WILL. That's okay, take your time. (*Bends down to inspect a violet.*) Here's a pink one.
MELINDA. (*Off.*) A pink what?
WILL. Violet. Pink. I never saw one before.
MELINDA. I think I'm ready now. (*Will goes quickly, in anticipation, to bench* R. *and sits. Melinda enters* U. R. *She is wearing a graceful Juliet costume. She stands a second, watching Will, then runs toward him. Spins around—the skirt swings out—she is smiling.*)
WILL. (*Appreciatively.*) Yeah! Oh, yeah! You look like—you look——
MELINDA. How?
WILL. That if somebody was sick and they saw you in it, they'd get all better.
MELINDA. No one has seen it yet. My mother only finished it last night. I wanted you to see it first. Do I look the way Juliet is supposed to?
WILL. Yeah. And when you say the lines at rehearsals you're getting to sound as if you really mean them.
MELINDA. Oh, yes, I mean them. Even the ones I don't understand, I mean them anyway. (*Walks front, looks out. Holding in*

her joyousness . . . scarcely able to believe it.) Springtime is nice for a town. Smell the lilacs.
WILL. (*Smiles at her imaginings.*) They're miles away.
MELINDA. They're sweet just the same. I'd like to smother my face in them. Drink them even. (*She turns to him quickly, enthusiastically.*) I wonder what it's like to get drunk. Were you ever?
WILL. No, but I think you forget about everything. You feel funny.
MELINDA. It's strange how you feel sometimes. Do you ever feel breathless, as if you've been running, when you haven't been running at all? Do you?
WILL. Yes. Sometimes.
MELINDA. (*Turns front, feeling breathless. Sees the violet.*) Oh, I see that violet. (*She goes front, down on her knees, looking at it. Softly.*) It must be sad to be a flower and be tramped on.
WILL. (*Walks down front. Squats down beside her, looking at the flower.*) They don't know.
MELINDA. (*Looks at him.*) We wouldn't either if we were killed, but it's nice not being.
WILL. (*Looks at her directly, understanding her meaning.*) Yeah. (*Their eyes hold for a second. His gaze is serious and steady, but hers falters. She drops her eyes, stands up, fearful of emotion. Looks down at her dress . . . smooths it.*)
MELINDA. I'm glad you like my dress.
WILL. Yeah, you really look like an actress when you're dressed up like that. Why don't you recite something for me in it?
MELINDA. (*Hesitates for a second, then runs up onto the bandstand. She stands behind the railing, looks down at him, thinks a moment, and then recites, very nicely and simply.*)

The face of the night when you see it close in the dark
May be lonely or troubled or asking
Questions with sad answers

And you look in the eyes of the stranger and search for despair
But instead it's the face of a friend and you see courage there.

Now the heat of the day is worn and so is the anger
For hatred is weak and forlorn and has to sleep;
But love can rest in the sun, or laugh, or weep,

And the strength of it lingers with silent might in the moon's cool light.

And love is what brings the courage to the face of the night.

WILL. That's one of my poems.
MELINDA. I like it the best. You wrote it a long time ago though. You promised to write another one. One especially for me.
WILL. That one's for you.
MELINDA. But you didn't know me when you wrote it.
WILL. (*In a very ordinary tone.*) Yeah, I knew you. I think I knew you all right.
MELINDA. It's funny how you can know things, isn't it? My mother and father weren't married to each other.
WILL. Who told you?
MELINDA. Nobody. It's one of the things I understand all of a sudden. (*She runs down from the bandstand.*) And square roots. That came to me yesterday, in Algebra. It's taken all these years. I'm terrible at Mathematics.
WILL. You're good in the play though.
MELINDA. (*Goes to bandstand, suddenly feeling like "somebody." With the air of a great lady, gracefully, she sits on the steps, spreading her skirts.*) I think I'd like to be an actress for a living.
WILL. That's all right, I guess. You'd be a pretty good one too. You'd have to travel a lot though.
MELINDA. I'd like that.
WILL. What about your husband?
MELINDA. My—husband?
WILL. Would you take him around with you?
MELINDA. If he'd like it.
WILL. He probably wouldn't.
MELINDA. (*A pause.*) Then I'd stay home with him.
WILL. (*Walks over to her.*) Would you like a stick of gum?
MELINDA. All right. (*He offers her the package, she takes a piece.*) Thank you very much.
WILL. (*Takes a piece himself. Puts package in his pocket. Unwraps gum, puts it in his mouth.*) Do you believe in God? (*He goes back to bench* R., *and sits.*)

MELINDA. (*Has started to unwrap gum. She stops.*) Why, of course I do. Don't you?
WILL. I'm on and off about that. We always go to church on Sunday and all that, and they say God is there and I always used to believe it when I was a little kid. And then one day I went into a church, it wasn't any special day, I think it was a Thursday. There weren't any people in there, and it didn't seem as if God was either.
MELINDA. (*Unwraps her gum, puts it in mouth.*) Oh, He must have been.
WILL. Well, maybe He was. It didn't feel like it though. I seem to believe in Him sometimes though. This week, for instance.
MELINDA. I don't think He'd like you going back and forth like that.
WILL. Oh, I guess he wouldn't mind. He'd probably understand. (*He has been tossing the rumpled gum paper up and down in his hand. Now, with a gay boyish gesture, he flips it around behind him, curving it so that it lands on the ground in front of him. Melinda watches him do it, and then, with solemn concentration, she does the same with her gum paper. They glance at each other with a little smile of camaraderie. Will heaves a big sigh of contentment, looks front at the town.*) I think I'd like to have a house some day in this town.
MELINDA. What kind of house?
WILL. A brick one. With storm windows and a furnace to look after, and a twenty year mortgage.
MELINDA. Wouldn't it be better to own it?
WILL. (*Firmly.*) I'd rather have a mortgage. What kind of a house would you like to live in best?
MELINDA. A castle.
WILL. Would you?
MELINDA. Oh—it was silly to say that. I didn't mean ——
WILL. That's okay. Some people live in castles. They'd be a nice place for children to play in. Do you like children?
MELINDA. Oh, I love them! (*A pause.*) Do you?
WILL. Not much.
MELINDA. Oh.
WILL. I could get used to them, I guess. I had a little brother once. Only he died. I liked him quite a lot.
MELINDA. What did he die of?

51

WILL. He got hit—by a moving van.
MELINDA. (*Gets up and crosses to him.*) Then you've been lonely.
WILL. (*Without sorrow.*) Kind of. I guess so.
MELINDA. (*Tentatively.*) There's a place to swim in the summertime. I'll show you.
WILL. I like to swim.
MELINDA. So do I. Usually the summer seems long—but it won't, this year. (*A little pause.*) I'd better change and we'll go home now. (*She goes* U. C., *then turns.*) I like brick houses the best too. (*Will watches her, very still, as she exits* U. R. *A pause. He turns away and begins to whistle. A bird joins in, and Will stops. Watches the bird, smiles. Melinda, off* R.) Do you know what, Will?
WILL. What?
MELINDA. At school, everyone is nice to me. Even Polly. Do you suppose it's because I'm in the play?
WILL. No, I don't think so. (*He gets up, wanders* D. S., *kicking experimentally at the ground.*)
MELINDA. Then why do you suppose it is?
WILL. Why wouldn't they be nice to you?
MELINDA. They never were before.
WILL. Well—they're funny, the kids. They like you if you're the same as them. It doesn't mean a heck of a lot. (*He glances up, and stiffens a bit as he sees someone approaching from* R.)
MELINDA. (*A pause.*) It does to me. Do you think that's terrible? I'm more like them, being in something. (*Polly appears from* R., *swinging a basket. She sees Will and waves. Will does not respond—just watches her as she comes down toward him.*)
POLLY. Hi, Will.
WILL. Hello.
MELINDA. I won't be long—it's just there are so many buttons.
POLLY. (*Only a slight stillness betrays her thought.*) Is that Melinda? You're both here. Isn't it a simply heavenly place?
WILL. Yeah.
POLLY. (*Smiles.*) I'm sorry if I interrupted you at a picnic or anything. I come up here sometimes in the spring—the violets grow here better than anywhere.
MELINDA. (*Still off.*) Is that someone there?
POLLY. (*Walks front, looks out.*) My goodness, doesn't the

school look ridiculous, perched on the edge of the hill. Everyone takes school so seriously.
MELINDA. (*Enters, now dressed in street clothes. She carries her costume. Senses a threat.*) Polly. Why are you here?
POLLY. Hello, Melinda. What's that you've got?
MELINDA. Polly—it's my costume —— (*She comes down.*)
POLLY. Oh, may I see it? (*Melinda holds it out, watches Polly's face.*) Oh, it looks lovely. Did your mother make it? (*She holds it up against herself with a quietly restrained longing.*)
MELINDA. Yes.
POLLY. Isn't she clever! And I've been wanting to tell you what a perfectly marvelous job I think you're doing in the play. I've been watching the rehearsals, and really and truly, Melinda, I've been simply amazed and so has everyone else.
MELINDA. (*With a rush of gratitude.*) Oh, Polly ——
POLLY. Will, aren't you terribly proud of her too?
MELINDA. Oh, Polly, I'm so sorry! I didn't know you wanted the part. I just went and tried out for it because Miss Robson asked me, and then I saw you there ——
POLLY. (*Smiling. Easily.*) I didn't *want* it, silly. My goodness, I've played the leads every year and it's got to be a bore. My mother's going to come anyway. She loves coming to school activities. Will your mother be coming to see you in the play?
MELINDA. Why, I —— (*A slight impasse, as they look at each other.*)
WILL. (*Crosses to Polly. Quietly.*) It's time I took Melinda home now. I'll take the dress.
POLLY. You're awfully nice to Melinda, Will. The way you come to all the rehearsals and everything. I always see you. I always see you being nice to her. (*She slowly holds out the dress, watching his face.*)
WILL. Come on, Melinda. (*He has been very still and on guard. Now he takes Melinda's hand and they start up.*)
POLLY. (*Seeing violets around the edge of bandstand.*) Here are some more violets. They're for my mother to wear tomorrow night. For Parents' Night. Is your mother coming to Parents' Night, Will? (*She is on her knees, inspecting the violets.*)
WILL. (*Over his shoulder.*) Yeah, I guess so. (*Melinda stops, turning front to Polly.*)
POLLY. My mother and father will be there too. They wouldn't

miss it for anything. They're so interested in everything I do. Isn't it nice to have your parents interested?
MELINDA. (*Suddenly.*) My mother's going too!
POLLY. (*Quietly.*) Is she?
MELINDA. (*Desperately . . . strengthening the decision.*) Yes—like everyone else.
POLLY. (*Speaks with warm generosity.*) Do you want some violets for her?
MELINDA. (*Starts over, feeling their friendship solidified.*) Oh, yes! (*Bends down to pick flowers.*)
POLLY. (*Has been picking violets.*) Look at this funny pink one. (*She plucks it out roughly and tosses it into her basket.*)
MELINDA. (*Stands slowly.*) No—you take the violets.
POLLY. There, that's enough. Well, let's go. (*Goes to Melinda, puts her arm around her waist.*) Oh, I have the best story to tell you, Melinda. You know Evelyn Pringle? Well, you'll positively die!
WILL. (*Walks over and quietly takes Melinda's hand, separating the two.*) Come on, Melinda. (*To Polly.*) I have to take Melinda home now. (*Will and Melinda exit U. R. Polly stands watching them go.*)

LIGHTS DIM TO BLACKOUT

ACT II

Scene 2

A pause, during which Melinda takes her place standing on a low stool in living room.
Lights come up on Grant living room, D. L. Mrs. Grant puts a full wrap-around skirt on Melinda, and starts pinning up hem. She goes down on her knees.

MELINDA. (*Is filled with suppressed excitement.*) You remember, don't you, Mother? I told you about it. I was so proud of Polly, and I used to imagine she was my friend. And now she is!
MRS. GRANT. (*Smiles.*) Yes, sweetheart. She's your very best friend.

MELINDA. (*Turns abruptly. Faces her.*) But, Mother, it's true. It's true, Mother! Now everything's different.
MRS. GRANT. (*Slowly.*) *You're* different ——
MELINDA. (*Drops to her knees, on stool, facing her.*) Oh, I knew you'd understand. Mother, I'm proud of you too—the lovely costume—I showed it to Polly, and she said you were very clever. She's always talking about her mother, and how important she is with her clubs and good works, but she said my mother was clever! They'll all think that when they see the rest of the costumes. And —when they see you.
MRS. GRANT. I can't pin the hem unless you stand up.
MELINDA. (*Stands, but not on the stool. Slowly and carefully.*) Tomorrow night, Mother, they're all coming to the school. They call it Parents' Night. All the parents come.
MRS. GRANT. That's nice.
MELINDA. Oh, yes, it's very nice! Nothing—nothing happens to worry about. Everybody puts on their best dress and they go to the Assembly Hall or they see around the school. You don't have to talk to anyone if you don't want to. Just be there, that's all. (*She is trying not to frighten her mother, and thereby risk a refusal. But she is in a fever of excitement and longing. Mrs. Grant knows that something terrible is happening, and she is very quiet and absolutely terrified.*)
MRS. GRANT. (*Pause.*) Parents' Night?
MELINDA. At my school. You've never seen my school, and you'll know what I'm talking about after this when I tell you things. You like me telling you about school, don't you, Mother?
MRS. GRANT. I like it sometimes. But I want to do your hem.
MELINDA. We'll do the hem in a minute. First, let's decide what you'll wear. Your green dress—you look the very prettiest in your green dress!
MRS. GRANT. I wear that to church.
MELINDA. (*Urgently.*) Yes, and you like going to church, don't you? Everyone is nice to you—you say good morning, and they all smile and are polite the way they say good morning back. Well, it'll be exactly the same tomorrow, only it'll be evening instead.
MRS. GRANT. I'll say "good evening."
MELINDA. (*Goes down on her knees on the floor.*) Yes! Yes! And I'll stay right beside you the way I do at church. Mother, you'll see how nice everyone is to me!

MRS. GRANT. Why are you different, Melinda?
MELINDA. But I'm not! I always thought I was, but now I'm just the same.
MRS. GRANT. (*Piteously.*) I don't understand, I don't understand.
MELINDA. You don't have to. You only have to stay beside me and do what I say, and we'll have such a good time.
MRS. GRANT. (*A whisper.*) All right.
MELINDA. (*Stands. Looks front, her face exultant.*) I didn't know I could be happy.
MRS. GRANT. (*Working on hem, even though Melinda is not on the stool. She has to work down close to the floor, and she gives the impression of someone broken and beaten.*) Why, you've always been happy.
MELINDA. No, I never have been. But now I'm happy all of the day and in the night too when I'm asleep. Isn't it strange that I'm not even afraid it'll go away. It couldn't go away. It couldn't, could it, Mother? (*Turns and looks at her mother. She sees fear, and becomes fearful.*) All you have to do is say good evening. and if they say anything else to you, like questions, then I'll answer for you. They'll just think you're shy. (*Leans down quickly, puts her arms around her mother and kisses her.*) Oh, Mother, I love you so much! (*There is no love, but only a passionate intensity about this outburst.*)
MRS. GRANT. You never said that to me before. (*She begins to sob, clutching Melinda around the knees.*)
MELINDA. (*Tightly.*) Don't—don't ——
MRS. GRANT. I don't like the way you are. You frighten me.
MELINDA. (*Breaking away.*) Oh, don't be frightened. I don't want you to be frightened, because we don't have to be . . . Oh, can't you understand?
MRS. GRANT. I don't understand anything.
MELINDA. (*In a fury of despair.*) Then try! You never even try! You only give up all the time and lean on me and lean on me and make me tired! (*She turns away, goes to window, stands looking out.*)
MRS. GRANT. (*A whisper.*) You're angry now.
MELINDA. (*Her back to her mother, her voice empty.*) No, I'm not. I'm not anything.
MRS. GRANT. (*Struggling up off her knees.*) You are, you are,

you're angry. Tell me what you want me to do, and I'll do it, Melinda. Just don't be angry. (*She goes to Melinda, her hands out beseechingly.*)
MELINDA. (*Swings on her.*) I want you to go to the school tomorrow night, and not be frightened! I want you never to be frightened!
MRS. GRANT. (*Terrified.*) Yes, dear, I'll never be frightened.
MELINDA. You'll go to the school!
MRS. GRANT. Yes ——
MELINDA. You promise!
MRS. GRANT. Yes!
MELINDA. And you won't go away anywhere and hide.
MRS. GRANT. No.
MELINDA. Promise.
MRS. GRANT. I promise. (*They stare at each other.*)

BLACKOUT

ACT II

Scene 3

A pause, and lights come up on section D. C. *It is a corridor of the High School, on Parents' Night. All entrances and exits are made from behind living room set* L., *or from behind kitchen set* R.
Eleanor dashes on from R., *followed by Anne.*

ELEANOR. (*Passionately.*) I hate her, I hate her, I hate her with all my heart!
ANNE. No you don't.
ELEANOR. I do!
ANNE. You only feel that way sometimes. I feel that way sometimes about my mother.
ELEANOR. She does it all the time—but in front of Mr. Bremner! I could die! And after he said—he said I was nice and neat. And then everyone heard her—she nearly shouted it. "You should just see her at home!" All she ever remembers is when I'm untidy, and she had to tell the whole school. (*She buries her face in her hands,*

sobs, and runs off L. *Anne stands watching. Miss Robson enters from* L.)
MISS ROBSON. What's going on out here? What's the matter with that girl?
ANNE. Nothing, Miss Robson.
MISS ROBSON. Every time I get nicely talking to a parent—one of you contradicts me or starts a racket—I wish some of you would try to understand. . . . Here's the key to Class C. I want the report cards, and watch that you turn on the light and not the fire alarm, it's right beside it.
ANNE. Yes, Miss Robson. (*Miss Robson starts back* L.) Miss Robson ——
MISS ROBSON. (*Turns.*) Yes, what is it? They're on the desk, you can't miss them.
ANNE. (*Goes to her.*) I just wondered —— You know where you helped me with my painting? With the forehead?
MISS ROBSON. (*Impatiently.*) No, I don't remember, dear.
ANNE. If my parents happen to ask you—it isn't that I lied to them, it's just that they think I did it myself. They're going to put it in the living room at home—they've just about decided—over the fireplace, right next to my sister's painting and she did every inch of hers herself. At least she says she did.
MISS ROBSON. Anne . . .
ANNE. (*Talking fast.*) And we're all very proud of Lucille. . . . I am too. But if they ask you about the painting . . .
MISS ROBSON. Anne, I have parents asking me right this minute about report cards, and I need those report cards! They're more recent than the art class, and you did very well in both, dear. (*She grips Anne's shoulders, smiles a quick, cheerful smile, and hurries off* L. *Anne walks slowly off* R. *Bruce enters* R. *Polly enters in pursuit.*)
POLLY. Bruce, I was talking to you!
BRUCE. I can't, Polly. (*Looks around in despair.*) Where did that tour get to?
POLLY. What tour?
BRUCE. The one I was conducting.
POLLY. (*Smiles, trying to be casual.*) Well, if you're not even interested in what I have to say . . .
BRUCE. (*Worried.*) Sure I'm interested. But couldn't it wait until tomorrow?

POLLY. I suppose so. It isn't very important. (*Walks* D. R., *not looking at him.*) It's only about the tennis matches. They're starting next week, you know.
MISS ROBSON. (*Off* L.) Bruce! (*Enters from* L.) Bruce Mitchell, I asked you to wait right here in the doorway of the Assembly Hall.
BRUCE. I'm sorry, Miss Robson, but I lost the tour.
MISS ROBSON. Lost it? How could you lose a tour? I had the whole evening beautifully planned, but everyone keeps moving around.
POLLY. Bruce and I were just talking for a minute.
MISS ROBSON. Polly, dear, is it too much to ask you that you consider your teachers for this one evening out of a year? That's three times this evening you've interrupted Bruce at things I want him to do. It isn't like you to be a nuisance. You're one of the people I *count* on! What is it that's troubling you?
POLLY. Oh, nothing! There isn't anything ——
MISS ROBSON. Yes, there is, my dear. I can tell by your face. (*Polly turns away. Miss Robson marches over to her.*) You've been looking very disturbed all evening. Don't think I don't notice these things. (*To Bruce.*) Bruce, have you been rude to Polly?
BRUCE. No, ma'am.
MISS ROBSON. Well, something is worrying her. (*To Polly.*) I'll give you a few seconds to continue your conversation, Polly. (*To Bruce.*) Bruce, I want you to show the Hendersons to the Music Room. Mrs. Henderson claims she used to play the harp and I think she's still interested in playing one. Please try to find a tactful way to keep her from trying it.
BRUCE. Yes, ma'am.
MISS ROBSON. (*Starts off. Turns to Polly.*) And remember, Polly. Today's little setbacks are tomorrow's triumphs! (*Exits* L.)
BRUCE. (*Is baffled.*) Did she say you were worrying about something? Something important?
POLLY. (*Very edgy.*) Of course it isn't important! I told you before it isn't important.
BRUCE. If it's only the tennis matches you're worrying about, well, I forgot they were starting, that's all.
POLLY. (*Angrily.*) You didn't forget other years! But you weren't playing in love scenes with Melinda Grant other years. Maybe you'd rather play tennis with her.

BRUCE. Who said anything about playing tennis with Melinda?
POLLY. Well, nobody said anything about playing it with me either. I'd appreciate it if you'd either get in your bid or drop out of the running!
BRUCE. I'm not running, kid. It seems to be you that's doing the running. (*Polly steps back, stunned.*) You're always making cracks about Melinda. As though she had leprosy or something. She's a nice kid. She's *nice!* The other day I got ashamed the way everybody's been to her. . . . Yeah, weren't you ever ashamed about anything? (*Polly turns away, holding back tears. The Hendersons enter* L.)
MISS ROBSON. (*Off* L.) You'll find Bruce waiting for you out in the hall.
MRS. HENDERSON. Thank you, Miss Robson. I'm anxious to see the Music Room. Oh, good evening. You'll be Bruce—Bruce Mitchell?
BRUCE. Yeah ——
MRS. HENDERSON. (*Crosses* C. *to him.*) I'm Will Henderson's mother. (*An afterthought.*) And this is Mr. Henderson.
BRUCE. How do you do.
MR. HENDERSON. Your father's chairman of the school board, isn't he, boy?
BRUCE. Yes, sir.
MR. HENDERSON. I nearly met him out on the golf course the other day, but he got away from me.
MRS. HENDERSON. (*Closing in.*) Tell me, Bruce. I'm sure you can tell me. How is Will getting along?
BRUCE. Will? He gets on okay, I guess.
MRS. HENDERSON. I mean, with you boys. You see, I worry about it. He doesn't talk much at home—you know how boys are—well, you're a boy yourself.
BRUCE. Yes, ma'am.
MRS. HENDERSON. (*Pleading.*) Will is quiet, and he's shy, but I wish you'd take the trouble to understand him, Bruce.
BRUCE. (*Embarrassed.*) Yeah, I guess so. Miss Robson said you'd like to see the Music Room.
MRS. HENDERSON. We'd like that very much. It's wonderful the way the schools are going in for music and the finer things these days. When I was a girl we had to get all that at home. You young people don't know how lucky you are. Come along, Ed.

MR. HENDERSON. (*As they start* R.) Your father here tonight, Bruce?
BRUCE. Yes, sir.
MR. HENDERSON. Well, maybe we'll run into him. (*They exit* R. *Polly is standing perfectly still. Anne rushes on from* L.)
ANNE. Polly, have you seen my mother and father?
POLLY. (*Rudely.*) No, why should I?
ANNE. What's the matter? Have you lost your parents too?
POLLY. You talk about losing your parents as if you were three years old!
ANNE. (*Puzzled, stares at her.*) Well, it's only I want to show them my painting. You know how parents are, thinking their children have artistic talent and making a big fuss over a thing like a painting. They just wanted to see it, that's all.
POLLY. (*Takes her hand and starts leading her* R.) Come on, let's go and get a soda.
ANNE. (*Pulling back.*) We couldn't just leave. What would your mother say?
POLLY. (*Lets her hand go.*) What's that got to do with anything? Besides, she isn't here. She's starting a traveling library for unfortunate cripples and things like that.
ANNE. Oh, that's too bad. Couldn't your father come?
POLLY. An important person like a doctor? Good heavens, he's too busy to come to a childish affair like this. My father's . . .
ANNE. (*Looking around.*) I'm sorry, Polly, but I've got to find my parents. (*Anne starts off,* L. *Meets Melinda and Mrs. Grant, who are just entering from* L.)
MELINDA. (*Eagerly.*) Anne—hello, Anne.
MRS. GRANT. (*Smiles.*) Good evening. (*She is dressed in her Sunday clothes, and they are awful. She's trying very hard, and looks pitifully out of place.*)
ANNE. (*Politely, trying to hide her wariness.*) Hello.
MELINDA. (*Convincing herself it's going fine.*) Anne, it's my mother. Mother, this is Anne.
MRS. GRANT. (*Repeating mechanically.*) Good evening.
ANNE. I'm glad to meet you, Mrs. Grant. Well—good-bye. I've got to find my parents. (*She runs off* L.)
MELINDA. (*Starts* R. *toward Polly.*) Oh, Polly. Oh, Polly, I've been looking all over for you. Isn't it lovely?
POLLY. (*Rudely.*) Isn't what lovely?

MELINDA. Why—everything. You know—everyone being here, and ——
MRS. GRANT. (*To Polly, smiling.*) Good evening. (*Polly glances at her, does not answer.*)
MELINDA. Polly, it's—it's my mother. I'd like you to meet her because —— Well, and I'd like to meet your parents too, Polly. Where are they?
POLLY. (*Intensely.*) How would I know where they are? Everybody's lost tonight, nobody knows where anybody else is, and all they can think of to do is ask me. (*She runs off* R.)
MRS. GRANT. (*Lost . . . amazed.*) Was that Polly?
MELINDA. Yes. She—sometimes she's very busy. Come on, we'll go and see the garden now.
MRS. GRANT. Is there a garden?
MELINDA. (*As they start* R.) Yes, and it's nice and quiet out there. It's ——
MR. HENDERSON. (*Off* R.) Well, can we see the gymnasium now?
WILL. (*Off* R.) Yes, it's right this way. (*The Hendersons enter from* R. *Melinda and Will look at each other . . . aware of each other's parents.*)
MELINDA. (*Tentatively . . . to Will, but including his parents.*) Hello. . . .
MRS. GRANT. Good evening. (*Mrs. Henderson has realized who they are. She lifts her head, walks past them. Mr. Henderson, embarrassed, starts to cross, stops in front of Mrs. Grant, nods, and crosses* L. *Will hesitates a moment. Mr. and Mrs. Henderson exit* L.)
WILL. Hello, Melinda.
MELINDA. Hello. Mother, this is a boy I know. His name is Will.
WILL. How do you do, Mrs. Grant.
MRS. GRANT. He looks like a nice boy. (*She turns front, fearfully.*)
MELINDA. Oh, yes, he is! (*She is embarrassed in front of Will. There is a sound of a young girl's sobbing from the shadows* R.)
MRS. GRANT. (*With an inner trembling.*) Someone is crying.
WILL. I like the costume you made for Melinda.
MRS. HENDERSON. (*Calling from off* L.) Will!
WILL. I guess I'll have to be going now.

MRS. GRANT. (*Urgently.*) Who is crying?
MELINDA. (*Tensing up.*) I don't know. . . .
WILL. (*Starts L. Stops. Sincerely.*) I'm glad I met you, Mrs. Grant.
MRS. GRANT. (*Clutches at Melinda. Frantically.*) Melinda, *who is crying?*
MELINDA. I don't know, Mother. . . . Nobody. . . . It doesn't matter. (*Hurriedly leads her R.*) Come and let me show you the garden. (*She gives Will a quick look, which pleads for understanding and exits with her mother R. Will watches them go . . . is torn. He changes his mind about joining his parents, and starts R. across stage.*)
MR. HENDERSON. (*Calling from off L.*) Will! (*Will quickens his pace across stage. Appears at L.*) Will!
WILL. (*Turns.*) Yeah . . . Dad . . . I was just coming. (*Discouraged, he starts across L.*)
MR. HENDERSON. (*Not unkindly.*) Your mother's waiting.
WILL. I know. (*They exit L. Voices are heard. Polly and Melinda enter R.*)
MELINDA. Of course I like talking to you, Polly. But couldn't we have talked out in the garden?
POLLY. Your mother will be all right, Melinda.
MELINDA. I know she will. But maybe she'll wonder why I left so quickly. Why were you hiding out there?
POLLY. I wasn't hiding.
MELINDA. And I thought you seemed to be crying too.
POLLY. (*Laughs.*) What a silly little thing you are. But I like you anyway, Melinda. I'm going to have a party soon, a big party, and I'd like you to come.
MELINDA. I'd love to.
POLLY. And then the boys will ask you out ——
MELINDA. I don't care about that.
POLLY. Of course not. You've got Will, haven't you? I guess you and Will are terribly in love.
MELINDA. Oh, no, Polly, it isn't anything like that.
POLLY. Isn't it?
MELINDA. Polly, will you come to my house too?
POLLY. I'd adore to. We'll go back and forth. That's what friends are for, isn't it, Melinda, to share things back and forth.
MELINDA. (*Eagerly.*) Oh, yes!

POLLY. (*A pause . . . she crosses* L. *Carefully.*) Melinda. You know what you said, up on the bandstand? You said you thought I wanted the part of Juliet . . .
MELINDA. . . . Yes . . .
POLLY. And I said I didn't care about playing Juliet. Well, that was only because I—I wasn't sure if you were my friend or not.
MELINDA. (*Slight pause.*) Oh.
POLLY. (*Comes toward her.*) Because the truth of the matter is, I would like to play Juliet, because I happen to have a more or less personal reason. I guess if you'd known I really wanted the part, you wouldn't have accepted it, would you?
MELINDA. (*Backs up a step.*) Why, I ——
POLLY. (*Follows her.*) Would you, Melinda! Not if I was your friend, and you knew I wanted it. That's what you said—you said that yesterday. You said you were sorry. Well, if you're really sorry—if you dropped out now for some reason—there are lots of reasons you could drop out—the rehearsals have barely started, and I know the whole part off by heart. (*She talks fast and breathlessly.*) It must be a bore for you anyway, having to rehearse every day when Will is waiting for you. To go up to the bandstand. Doesn't he, Melinda? Doesn't he wait for you every day, and you go up there together!
MELINDA. No—not every day ——
POLLY. (*Intensely.*) Yes! Every day! It's every day, and I know, because I've seen you.
MELINDA. (*Frightened.*) Polly—if you would just ——
POLLY. (*Now she smiles.*) But we don't have to argue about it anyway. All I want is for you to drop out of the play, and then we'll never have to mention the bandstand again.
MELINDA. I couldn't. I couldn't do that, Polly. I wouldn't have any reason to drop out of the play.
POLLY. (*Her voice hard.*) I just told you the reason.
MELINDA. You're only teasing, aren't you, Polly? My mother has made nearly all the costumes. And Mr. Chesley wouldn't understand. How could he? I don't understand. I don't understand at all why you'd—unless —— You were crying outside. Why, Polly? Is it because your mother didn't come tonight?
POLLY. (*A tortured cry.*) Shut up!
MELINDA. Polly ——
POLLY. Shut up, shut up!

MELINDA. Yes, it is. I understand about some things. You picked some violets for your mother.
POLLY. (*Looks front. In wonderment.*) She didn't even put them in water . . . just left them lying on the kitchen table till they were dead. That's what they'd like me to be—my parents—dead.
MELINDA. No, they wouldn't.
POLLY. (*Swings on her.*) What do you know about it? Your mother wouldn't come to the play anyhow. But mine would, and so would my father. They'd bring all their friends, and they'd look at me and see me there. Please, Melinda. Please, please. I'll do anything for you. Please let me be in the play. It's easy for you.
MELINDA. No it isn't.
POLLY. (*Pleading piteously.*) Please!
MELINDA. I can't—I can't—I want to be your friend, but ——
POLLY. (*Suddenly in a fury.*) My friend! Would you like to know something, Melinda Grant? I've never hated anybody in this whole world as much as I hate you. (*Melinda steps back. Polly follows.*) I'll give you one last chance. You drop out of that play or I'll tell everybody everything about you and Will Henderson!
MELINDA. There isn't anything to tell!
POLLY. There's plenty. There's lots to tell. And I'll start tonight —right away—and you'll be sorry, you'll be sorry ——
MELINDA. Stop it! Don't you talk to me any more! Just don't you ever talk to me again. You said you were my friend. You don't know what it means to have a friend. You must never have had a friend.
POLLY. (*Almost hysterically.*) You—you—*slut!* (*She turns and runs off* L. *Melinda stands, staring front.*)
WILL. (*Off* L.) Melinda. (*He enters quickly.*) Say, listen, Melinda, I'm sorry about my parents—the way they were —— (*Melinda turns slowly to face him.*) It doesn't matter, Melinda. I thought your mother was nice, and it doesn't matter what anybody thinks!
MELINDA. (*Staring at him.*) Yes, it does.
WILL. No, it never does.
MELINDA. They think things about us too.
WILL. About who?
MELINDA. Us.
WILL. How do you mean? What do they think? (*Melinda drops*

her face into her hands.) Melinda——? (*Melinda shakes her head.*) What's the matter? (*Bruce strolls casually on stage from* L. *Will turns to look at him.*)
BRUCE. Hi, Will.
WILL. Hello.
BRUCE. I guess I've been wrong about you. (*He's smiling . . . and he's hurt.*) And about her, too.
WILL. Who?
BRUCE. Funny how you can be wrong about people. But I guess you knew about her right from the start.
WILL. What do you mean, anyway?
BRUCE. (*Looks around him . . . at Melinda.*) Wanta take a little walk up to the bandstand sometime, Melinda? Seems you and your mother prefer travellers, but there's a lot of good in the old home town boys.
WILL. (*A low passionate cry.*) Oh, you son of a bitch! (*With a sob, he leaps at Bruce, swinging with everything. Bruce goes down, and Will is on top of him.*)

BLACKOUT

ACT III

Scene 1

Lights come up on the Henderson kitchen, D. S. R. Mrs. Henderson sits at kitchen table with magazines spread before her, looking through them. Glances at her watch, flips some pages restlessly. She hears a step, goes quickly to door. Opens it. Mr. Henderson enters. He doesn't look at her. Slowly takes off his coat, hangs it on hook by door, sits at other side of table, arms hanging limp.

MRS. HENDERSON. Did you see them?
MR. HENDERSON. Yeah.
MRS. HENDERSON. What happened?
MR. HENDERSON. Talk. Lots of talk. Everybody talks too much, everybody in the world. You ever notice how everybody's mouth is always flapping all the time and nothing comes out but talk?
MRS. HENDERSON. (*Leans over table.*) All right, Ed, but what happened?
MR. HENDERSON. Bruce Mitchell's okay. His nose is broken. (*He gets up, goes to refrigerator. Peers inside, takes out a bottle of beer.*) His old man said ten thousand million words about what a fine shape nose he used to have and now it's ruined since last night, and then he said it doesn't matter about his nose. It's the principle of the thing that matters. What's this goddam principle everybody's always talking about? (*Has opened beer, now sits, tips up bottle, and drinks.*)
MRS. HENDERSON. (*In disgust.*) Use a glass, Ed.
MR. HENDERSON. (*Holds out bottle and studies it.*) I saw a guy get hit with one of these things once. Bottle smashed in a million pieces and all that happened to his nose was a scratch. (*Looks up at her, pleased.*) I never would've thought our boy could pack a wallop like that. Fancy that kid turning out to be a fighter. I'm proud of him, Dorothy, now that's the truth, I'm

proud of him. (*Gets up, goes toward her, his voice hard.*) And I don't want you nagging at him, get that, Dorothy, what's done is done, so leave him alone!

MRS. HENDERSON. (*Turns away . . . few steps* L.) You're talking a lot, Ed. You haven't said anything.

HENDERSON. He's expelled.

MRS. HENDERSON. Expelled?

MR. HENDERSON. (*Spelling it.*) E-x ——

MRS. HENDERSON. (*Goes toward him. Ferociously.*) They expelled him because he got into a little fight?

MR. HENDERSON. They expelled him because of principle! That's what I've just been explaining to you. They explained it all to me good and careful, and Mitchell's nose doesn't even enter into the picture. (*Smiles.*) He broke it in six places. I wonder if he did that with one punch?

MRS. HENDERSON. (*Sinks into a chair. Slowly.*) So you're proud of him.

MR. HENDERSON. (*The smile is gone.*) I'm not proud of him. I'm ashamed, sick, I'd like to kill him. (*He stands quickly, looks about, smashes the beer bottle into the sink. Stands with his back to audience, as the passion drains out of him.*) That girl . . . that girl . . .

MRS. HENDERSON. What about her?

MR. HENDERSON. I never minded him being the way he was. I could always know he was a good kid, I could fall back on that. (*Bewildered, turns.*) I always thought he was moral.

MRS. HENDERSON. Certainly he's moral.

MR. HENDERSON. (*Coming down from sink. Angrily.*) No, he isn't moral. Him and that girl he fought over—they've been up to things.

MRS. HENDERSON. What things? (*Quickly.*) Who told you a thing like that?

MR. HENDERSON. They did—the school board bunch. It's that, they said, not Mitchell's nose. It's Will's morals, and she was a fine innocent girl till he come along. It made me sick to my stomach.

MRS. HENDERSON. Do you think it's true?

MR. HENDERSON. What if it is true? He's seventeen—at least he's normal!—Listen, Dorothy, there's only one thing I ask of you. Don't say anything right now about your father. That's all. Now that isn't very much to ask, is it? Go ahead and cry, cry all you

want. That is if you have to. (*A pause.*) Do you think you're going to cry?
MRS. HENDERSON. (*Slowly.*) So it was on account of that girl. He's known her a month. A girl he's known thirty days.
MR. HENDERSON. (*Goes to sink and starts picking up pieces of glass. Looks back with a grin.*) Now that showed real presence of mind, don't you think so, throwing it in the sink? Would've been a hell of a mess to sweep up.
MRS. HENDERSON. I wanted so much for him.
MR. HENDERSON. They sure do use lousy glass in these bottles. It's practically powdered.
MRS. HENDERSON. For seventeen years I've planned the very best for him. To get away from all this. To have all the things we've never had. I expected so much from him. And now, because of that girl, that girl that he's known a month. . . . And he never stopped for one minute to think of me.
MR. HENDERSON. No, it isn't anything personal like that, kid ——
MRS. HENDERSON. I've always hoped he had some love in him for me. But I've known all along that he didn't. I've known about him, Ed, and I've known about you, too.
MR. HENDERSON. (*Blankly.*) Me?
MRS. HENDERSON. It's all right, Ed. I don't blame you. Either of you. (*Without emotion.*) No one has ever loved me one little bit in my whole life. Except my baby . . . and I can't even go to his grave because he's five stops behind us, or is it four stops. Anyway, it's where a moving van has blood on its wheels . . . (*She stops because she is overcome. But her sobbing is silent, it is deep within her.*)
MR. HENDERSON. I love you, Dorothy. (*He is heartbroken. Mrs. Henderson smiles.*) And so does Will. We couldn't get along without you. And your father, Dorothy. Your father loved you.
MRS. HENDERSON. (*With a great effort, she achieves calm.*) No, he didn't. My father didn't love a single living soul. I wanted him to love me and I worked at it all my life. He was always very nice to me. Very polite. Will is always polite to me. When he comes home this afternoon, I'll be polite to him too. I won't have to say a word about him disgracing us, because disgrace only matters if people are looking, and no one is looking, because we don't count. (*A deep sigh.*)

MR. HENDERSON. (*Lost.*) I guess I don't quite understand that.
MRS. HENDERSON. It's kind of a relief, Ed. Like getting to the end of a job that's been too hard to do anyway. Peaceful. Like dying. (*She is almost exultant with the peace and stillness that flood her spirit.*)
MR. HENDERSON. Are you going to cry now?
MRS. HENDERSON. No, I don't think I'm ever going to cry any more.
MR. HENDERSON. (*Feeling his feet on solid ground.*) That's real sensible, Dorothy. And you're right, there's no use being hard on the boy. (*He turns and starts picking up glass from sink.*)
MRS. HENDERSON. No, I won't be hard on him. Not ever again about anything. Here, I'll clean that up. (*She rises.*) You get yourself another beer.

LIGHTS DIM TO BLACKOUT

ACT III

Scene 2

A pause. Lights come up on the bandstand.
Will is alone on stage, sitting on the steps of the bandstand. The sky is overcast. A bird sings, but Will does not look at it. He is whittling. Melinda enters from R., *and although she makes no sound, he knows she is there. He stands. She walks down beside him, both looking at each other.*

MELINDA. Am I very late?
WILL. It's only about five o'clock.
MELINDA. I went straight home from school for a little while. My mother wanted me to.
WILL. Was she feeling bad after last night?
MELINDA. Yes.
WILL. Is she feeling any better now?
MELINDA. (*She is tense and fearful . . . watching his face for some signal.*) No. But I ran away from her. She was crying. I didn't care. I came up here. Have you been home?

WILL. Yeah. (*Bird sings. Will attempts cheerfulness.*) There's our bird. (*Both look up. Then Melinda goes to bench, R., and sits.*) Did anyone—did they say anything to you today?
MELINDA. No. Nobody said anything. (*Will whittles. She watches him.*) What are you making?
WILL. A sort of a little boat. It's the easiest thing to whittle. I never was very good at whittling. These boats, they're the easiest, and I never got past them. Here, would you like to have it? (*He is trying to steady her by sounding very normal and conversational.*)
MELINDA. (*As he walks over and hands it to her.*) Thank you.
WILL. (*Hesitates a moment.*) Would you like to have the penknife, too?
MELINDA. Why, that's very nice of you, but what would I use it for?
WILL. Well, for one thing, it has my initials on it. (*Sits on bench beside her.*) You see, right here?
MELINDA. (*As they bend over it.*) Oh, yes.
WILL. You could keep it as a—a kind of keepsake. And besides, I'm forever losing penknives. Gee, I must have lost two dozen penknives in my life. Well, this way, I'll know right where this one is. And some day I'll come back here, to this town, and I'll get it. (*Melinda looks up at him, her eyes pleading. She has gone rigid.*) I will, Melinda. I give you my word of honor I will. Listen—listen —we haven't got anything to worry about, see? Lots of people, they're together all the time, and they hate each other. Being together isn't everything in the world. It—it has a little blade at the other end that opens out—here, I'll show you. (*She hands him the knife. He opens it.*) It's extra sharp, and it's very good for pencils.
MELINDA. How soon will you be going away?
WILL. When my dad decides to move on, we get out right away. We don't take much stuff with us. We can pack it all in about a couple of hours.
MELINDA. When, Will?
WILL. Tonight. (*She stands.*) They knew I was coming here to see you, but they didn't say anything. They didn't even say to hurry. So we can plan things, Melinda.
MELINDA. There isn't anything to plan. (*She walks around, wavering a little, stiffly, as she struggles for control. She walks front, finally, and looks out and down.*) I used to plan sometimes.

I used to look at the cliff and plan terrible things. But I was afraid it would hurt. I don't think it would hurt very much.

WILL. (*Goes to her, speaking urgently and firmly.*) Coming up here, I started planning everything. Like writing to you, for instance. I'll write every day. Sometimes a person can tell another person lots more things in letters than they ever could really. (*She wanders away from him . . . up to bandstand, hardly hearing him, so great is her struggle. Then she turns and speaks desperately.*)

MELINDA. Do you have to do what they say?

WILL. For a little while.

MELINDA. I don't want you to go away.

WILL. After I finish school I can do what I want. The first thing I'll do is come back here, and then we'll plan everything else. I will come back, Melinda. I give you my word. So going away isn't so bad.

MELINDA. It's—terrible. (*She stands on the bandstand steps, facing front, holding onto the post.*)

WILL. Nothing is so very terrible. (*Cornet begins to play. He goes over to her, speaks honestly and forcefully.*) There was a house once down by a lake near where we used to live. The house was all boarded up and deserted, and the kids all said it was haunted and were afraid of it. I was too. More afraid than any of them. And then my mother and dad decided we'd live in that house, and I nearly ran away. I was going to, but I didn't. I decided to be brave, but I didn't know how I could do it I felt so sick. But I went inside that house and I looked at it, every bit of it, up close. It was just an ordinary old house and there I was being afraid of nothing at all. (*Melinda begins to cry, looking at him. The weeping becomes a tearing sobbing, and she puts her head down and continues to sob for a long time. She sinks down onto the steps. Will stands quietly, watching her. Once he starts to reach out his hand to her, but takes it back. When the crying has subsided a little.*) Some people say men don't like it when girls cry, but they're the kind of people that don't like girls to laugh either. Or anybody. I think if you can do one, then it's easier to do the other, and both of them make you feel good. Will you write to me too, Melinda, every day? You don't have to stop crying. Just nod.

MELINDA. (*With effort, she stops crying. Lifts her head.*) I'll cry later.
WILL. Okay. (*He sits beside her on the step.*)
MELINDA. Yes, I'll write to you.
WILL. And tell me all about the play? (*She nods.*) I think it's going to be a swell play. Don't—don't mind about Bruce—what he said. (*She shakes her head.*) See, it doesn't matter. It would only matter if it was true.
MELINDA. It was nice of you just the same, to defend me like that.
WILL. They say his nose is going to be bent. It's too bad I bent it, but that's another keepsake anyway. When you're doing the play, every time you look at Bruce's nose, you can think about me. (*Melinda laughs suddenly. Will smiles, but not at his joke.*)
MELINDA. They'll take pictures of the play, Mr. Chesley said. I'll send you one of me.
WILL. That would be nice. But it's best just to know you won't ever stop—writing—or anything.
MELINDA. Oh, no! Oh, I won't ever stop! I couldn't, not ever. Because ——
WILL. Why?
MELINDA. I can't ——
WILL. Because why?
MELINDA. I can't say it ——
WILL. Go on and say it!
MELINDA. I'll whisper it.
WILL. All right. (*She leans over and whispers.*) I'm glad. I knew you did.
MELINDA. You whisper it to me too.
WILL. I'll say it right out. (*Simply.*) I love you, Melinda.
MELINDA. I wonder why.
WILL. Because I seem to know you.
MELINDA. Say my name.
WILL. Melinda. (*She rises.*) Let's walk down the hill and into town like we do other evenings, and not say much of anything. And when we get to the corner where the candy store is, we'll just say good night. The way we always do. Just as if it's only good night until tomorrow.
MELINDA. All right. (*They stand, and as they do so, the little boat tumbles from her lap onto the ground. He picks it up and*

hands it to her. Takes her hand, and they start U. R. She stops a moment . . . turns to him. Her back and profile are to the audience.) Isn't it funny? All day, it seemed like just an ordinary day. (They exit, U. R., as:)

LIGHTS SLOWLY DIM TO BLACKOUT

(Cornet has been playing, and continues through pause, during which all of the stage is in darkness, and through following. Lights come up simultaneously on Grant living room and Henderson kitchen. Lights are not quite full. Mrs. Grant sits on the sofa, sewing. The Hendersons stand waiting in their kitchen, surrounded by packed suitcases. At the same moment, both children enter their homes. Melinda enters at far L., goes into living room, sits on the floor at her mother's feet. She remains there quietly, looking front. As Will enters the kitchen, U. R., his mother turns away. Mr. Henderson smiles at his son, puts a hand briefly on Will's shoulder, picks up two suitcases and exits. Will takes two suitcases and exits. Mrs. Henderson starts to leave. Then she stops. From a shopping bag which she's carrying, she takes some magazines. Walks over to waste basket and drops them into it. Exits without looking around. Lights out on kitchen. Up a little on Grant living room. Cornet out.)

ACT III

Scene 3

The Grant living room.

MRS. GRANT. (*Without looking up from her sewing.*) You haven't said anything for such a long time.
MELINDA. (*On floor at her mother's knee.*) I'm right here, though. (*Looking down at her hands. She is holding the little boat.*) There isn't anything to worry about.
MRS. GRANT. Oh, I'm not worried. When you were out, I finally remembered about last night. Melinda. I didn't go away last night. I promised you I wouldn't go away and hide. And I didn't. We were in the garden, and it was you went away from me.

MELINDA. Yes, I know. I'm sorry I went away and left you. I won't go away and leave you any more. Until I grow up and get married.
MRS. GRANT. Will you leave me then?
MELINDA. (*Kindly.*) I won't go far. I'll take care of you.
MRS. GRANT. (*A little fearfully.*) Where will you go?
MELINDA. (*More to herself than her mother. She makes the decision.*) I'll stay right here in this town.
MRS. GRANT. (*Comforted by the certainty of her tone.*) And we'll be friends with each other.
MELINDA. Yes.
MRS. GRANT. Melinda, I'm glad I saw your school. (*Sews.*)
MELINDA. I won't make you go there any more.
MRS. GRANT. Oh, thank you. Seeing it once is enough, isn't it? And I'll just wear my green dress to church. (*She is content. Melinda withdraws into her own thoughts again, turning the boat around in her hands. Mrs. Grant senses her withdrawal.*) Tell me something nice.
MELINDA. (*Slowly.*) Yes. There are nice things. (*Leans up eagerly to show her mother.*) I have a little boat.
MRS. GRANT. Something about school . . .
MELINDA. Sometimes. When nice things really happen—I will tell you. And in between, if you want a story, I'll tell you a story out of a book.
MRS. GRANT. Tell me a story now.
MELINDA. Well . . . there's the play I'm going to be in. It's about Romeo and Juliet.
MRS. GRANT. Who are they?
MELINDA. They love each other. (*She speaks very simply.*) Only their parents don't want them to see each other, but they do just the same. And they get to love each other more. And they're happy together, and all the world looks beautiful. But then it's very sad at the end of the story, because they get lost from each other. Not really lost, but for a while they think they are. And they want to die.
MRS. GRANT. (*Sewing.*) Do they die?
MELINDA. (*Looking front. Repeating.*) They want to die. It seems as though that would be the easiest. They're right, I guess. But after they're both dead, that's when it's the very saddest. Because if they only could have been braver they could have stayed

living, and they might have been happy again some day. It's harder that way though, so they didn't.

MRS. GRANT. It's very mixed up, isn't it? (*There is a rumble of thunder.*)

MELINDA. (*Stands.*) It's going to rain.

MRS. GRANT. Melinda . . . are you going to go out in it?

MELINDA. (*She has started toward the window. She hesitates, half drawn toward it, the old conflict returning for a moment.*) No . . . I was thinking . . . how nice it will be . . . for the flowers. (*She turns.*) I think I'll go up to my room though and write a letter.

MRS. GRANT. Like Miss Willer's friend. (*She stands looking at her mother quietly. Mrs. Grant speaks with love and tenderness. A touch of a mother's warmth.*) At the end of the letter . . . you will put . . . "love." (*There is a small halo around the word Love.*)

MELINDA. Yes. (*She and her mother have met for an instant for the first time. This is what leads her to the dolls. She goes and takes one up—hardly breathing.*)

MRS. GRANT. Are you going to play with it?

MELINDA. (*Starts up to the door. Does not look at her mother.*) I'm too old to play with them. But I'll put it on my bed and it will look nice there. (*At the door she turns. Looks at her mother.*) Mother.

MRS. GRANT. What?

MELINDA. You look very pretty this evening. (*She exits. Mrs. Grant faces front, smiles a little, then sews in perfect contentment. Lights dim slowly as:*)

THE CURTAIN FALLS

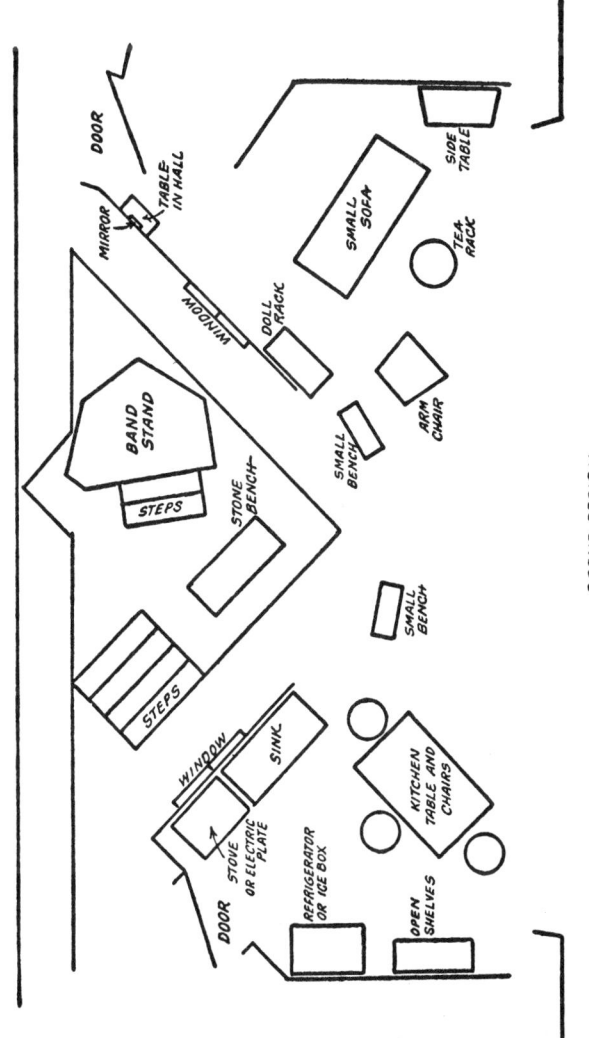

SCENE DESIGN
"TEACH ME HOW TO CRY"

PROPERTY PLOT

Act I—Scene 1

Grant Living Room D. L.:
Tea tray on tea rack before sofa. On it, two cups, milk, sugar, teapot, spoons
Off L.: Cup and saucer, white party dress
Mrs. Grant: Sewing

Scene 3

Henderson Kitchen D. R.:
Books, papers, pencils on kitchen table
3 places set for dinner at table—plates, silver, napkins, bread, butter, etc.
On stove: Pots and pans with stew and potatoes in them
On shelves R.: Bowls, magazines

Scene 4

Melinda: Book
Will: Coat or jacket, package of gum

Act II—Scene 1

Polly: Basket
Off R. for Melinda: Juliet costume, everyday dress

Scene 2

Put low stool C. in living room, D. L. area
Mrs. Grant: Full wrap-around skirt, pins

Act III—Scene 1

Henderson Living Room D. R.:
Magazines on kitchen table
Bottle of beer in ice box
Mr. Henderson: Coat

Scene 2

Small wooden boat, roughly carved; penknife

In Henderson Kitchen D. R.:
Suitcases on floor
Mrs. Henderson: Shopping bag with magazines in it

Scene 3

Mrs. Grant: Sewing

NEW PLAYS

★ **CLOSER by Patrick Marber.** Winner of the 1998 Olivier Award for Best Play and the 1999 New York Drama Critics Circle Award for Best Foreign Play. Four lives intertwine over the course of four and a half years in this densely plotted, stinging look at modern love and betrayal. "CLOSER is a sad, savvy, often funny play that casts a steely, unblinking gaze at the world of relationships and lets you come to your own conclusions ... CLOSER does not merely hold your attention; it burrows into you." –*New York Magazine* "A powerful, darkly funny play about the cosmic collision between the sun of love and the comet of desire." –*Newsweek Magazine* [2M, 2W] ISBN: 0-8222-1722-8

★ **THE MOST FABULOUS STORY EVER TOLD by Paul Rudnick.** A stage manager, headset and prompt book at hand, brings the house lights to half, then dark, and cues the creation of the world. Throughout the play, she's in control of everything. In other words, she's either God, or she thinks she is. "Line by line, Mr. Rudnick may be the funniest writer for the stage in the United States today ... One-liners, epigrams, withering put-downs and flashing repartee: These are the candles that Mr. Rudnick lights instead of cursing the darkness ... a testament to the virtues of laughing ... and in laughter, there is something like the memory of Eden." –*The NY Times* "Funny it is ... consistently, rapaciously, deliriously ... easily the funniest play in town." –*Variety* [4M, 5W] ISBN: 0-8222-1720-1

★ **A DOLL'S HOUSE by Henrik Ibsen, adapted by Frank McGuinness.** Winner of the 1997 Tony Award for Best Revival. "New, raw, gut-twisting and gripping. Easily the hottest drama this season." –*USA Today* "Bold, brilliant and alive." –*The Wall Street Journal* "A thunderclap of an evening that takes your breath away." –*Time Magazine* [4M, 4W, 2 boys] ISBN: 0-8222-1636-1

★ **THE HERBAL BED by Peter Whelan.** The play is based on actual events which occurred in Stratford-upon-Avon in the summer of 1613, when William Shakespeare's elder daughter was publicly accused of having a sexual liaison with a married neighbor and family friend. "In his probing new play, THE HERBAL BED ... Peter Whelan muses about a sidelong event in the life of Shakespeare's family and creates a finely textured tapestry of love and lies in the early 17th-century Stratford." –*The NY Times* "It is a first rate drama with interesting moral issues of truth and expediency." –*The NY Post* [5M, 3W] ISBN: 0-8222-1675-2

★ **SNAKEBIT by David Marshall Grant.** A study of modern friendship when put to the test. "... a rather smart and absorbing evening of water-cooler theater, the intimate sort of Off-Broadway experience that has you picking apart the recognizable characters long after the curtain calls." – *The NY Times* "Off-Broadway keeps on presenting us with compelling reasons for going to the theater. The latest is SNAKEBIT, David Marshall Grant's smart new comic drama about being thirtysomething and losing one's way in life." –*The NY Daily News* [3M, 1W] ISBN: 0-8222-1724-4

★ **A QUESTION OF MERCY by David Rabe.** The Obie Award-winning playwright probes the sensitive and controversial issue of doctor-assisted suicide in the age of AIDS in this poignant drama. "There are many devastating ironies in Mr. Rabe's beautifully considered, piercingly clear-eyed work ..." –*The NY Times* "With unsettling candor and disturbing insight, the play arouses pity and understanding of a troubling subject ... Rabe's provocative tale is an affirmation of dignity that rings clear and true." –*Variety* [6M, 1W] ISBN: 0-8222-1643-4

★ **DiMLY PERCEIVED THREATS TO THE SYSTEM by Jon Klein.** Reality and fantasy overlap with hilarious results as this unforgettable family attempts to survive the nineties. "Here's a play whose point about fractured families goes to the heart, mind – and ears." –*The Washington Post* "... an end-of-the-millennium comedy about a family on the verge of a nervous breakdown ... Trenchant and hilarious ..." –*The Baltimore Sun* [2M, 4W] ISBN: 0-8222-1677-9

DRAMATISTS PLAY SERVICE, INC.
440 Park Avenue South, New York, NY 10016 212-683-8960 Fax 212-213-1539
postmaster@dramatists.com   www.dramatists.com

NEW PLAYS

★ **AS BEES IN HONEY DROWN by Douglas Carter Beane.** Winner of the John Gassner Playwriting Award. A hot young novelist finds the subject of his new screenplay in a New York socialite who leads him into the world of *Auntie Mame* and *Breakfast at Tiffany's*, before she takes him for a ride. "A delicious soufflé of a satire ... [an] extremely entertaining fable for an age that always chooses image over substance." –*The NY Times* "... A witty assessment of one of the most active and relentless industries in a consumer society ... the creation of 'hot' young things, which the media have learned to mass produce with efficiency and zeal." –*The NY Daily News* [3M, 3W, flexible casting] ISBN: 0-8222-1651-5

★ **STUPID KIDS by John C. Russell.** In rapid, highly stylized scenes, the story follows four high-school students as they make their way from first through eighth period and beyond, struggling with the fears, frustrations, and longings peculiar to youth. "In STUPID KIDS ... playwright John C. Russell gets the opera of adolescence to a T ... The stylized teenspeak of STUPID KIDS ... suggests that Mr. Russell may have hidden a tape recorder under a desk in study hall somewhere and then scoured the tapes for good quotations ... it is the kids' insular, ceaselessly churning world, a pre-adult world of Doritos and libidos, that the playwright seeks to lay bare." –*The NY Times* "STUPID KIDS [is] a sharp-edged ... whoosh of teen angst and conformity anguish. It is also very funny." –*NY Newsday* [2M, 2W] ISBN: 0-8222-1698-1

★ **COLLECTED STORIES by Donald Margulies.** From Obie Award-winner Donald Margulies comes a provocative analysis of a student-teacher relationship that turns sour when the protégé becomes a rival. "With his fine ear for detail, Margulies creates an authentic, insular world, and he gives equal weight to the opposing viewpoints of two formidable characters." –*The LA Times* "This is probably Margulies' best play to date ..." –*The NY Post* "... always fluid and lively, the play is thick with ideas, like a stock-pot of good stew." –*The Village Voice* [2W] ISBN: 0-8222-1640-X

★ **FREEDOMLAND by Amy Freed.** An overdue showdown between a son and his father sets off fireworks that illuminate the neurosis, rage and anxiety of one family – and of America at the turn of the millennium. "FREEDOMLAND's more obvious links are to *Buried Child* and *Bosoms and Neglect*. Freed, like Guare, is an inspired wordsmith with a gift for surreal touches in situations grounded in familiar and real territory." –*Curtain Up* [3M, 4W] ISBN: 0-8222-1719-8

★ **STOP KISS by Diana Son.** A poignant and funny play about the ways, both sudden and slow, that lives can change irrevocably. "There's so much that is vital and exciting about STOP KISS ... you want to embrace this young author and cheer her onto other works ... the writing on display here is funny and credible ... you also will be charmed by its heartfelt characters and up-to-the-minute humor." –*The NY Daily News* "... irresistibly exciting ... a sweet, sad, and enchantingly sincere play." –*The NY Times* [3M, 3W] ISBN: 0-8222-1731-7

★ **THREE DAYS OF RAIN by Richard Greenberg.** The sins of fathers and mothers make for a bittersweet elegy in this poignant and revealing drama. "... a work so perfectly judged it heralds the arrival of a major playwright ... Greenberg is extraordinary." –*The NY Daily News* "Greenberg's play is filled with graceful passages that are by turns melancholy, harrowing, and often, quite funny." –*Variety* [2M, 1W] ISBN: 0-8222-1676-0

★ **THE WEIR by Conor McPherson.** In a bar in rural Ireland, the local men swap spooky stories in an attempt to impress a young woman from Dublin who recently moved into a nearby "haunted" house. However, the tables are soon turned when she spins a yarn of her own. "You shed all sense of time at this beautiful and devious new play." –*The NY Times* "Sheer theatrical magic. I have rarely been so convinced that I have just seen a modern classic. Tremendous." –*The London Daily Telegraph* [4M, 1W] ISBN: 0-8222-1706-6

DRAMATISTS PLAY SERVICE, INC.
440 Park Avenue South, New York, NY 10016 212-683-8960 Fax 212-213-1539
postmaster@dramatists.com www.dramatists.com